The Visionary Christian

THE VISIONARY

131 READINGS FROM

CHRISTIAN

C. S. Lewis

Selected and edited by Chad Walsh

COLLIER BOOKS
Macmillan Publishing Company
NEW YORK

ACKNOWLEDGMENTS

For permission to reprint materials, grateful acknowledgment is made to the following:

The Trustees of the Estate of C. S. Lewis, for excerpts from C. S. Lewis, *Spirits in Bondage* (published under the pseudonym of Clive Hamilton).
Wm. B. Eerdmans Publishing Co., for excerpts from C. S. Lewis, *The Pilgrim's Regress*, Copyright 1933 and 1943 by Clive Staples Lewis.
Harcourt Brace Jovanovich, Inc., for excerpts from C. S. Lewis, *Till We Have Faces*, © 1956 by C. S. Lewis; *Poems*, Copyright © 1964 by the Executors of the Estate of C. S. Lewis; *Narrative Poems*, Copyright © 1969 by The Trustees of the Estate of C. S. Lewis.
William Collins Sons & Co. Ltd., for excerpts from C. S. Lewis, *The Horse and His Boy*, Copyright 1954 by The Trustees of the Estate of C. S. Lewis; *Prince Caspian*, Copyright 1951 by The Trustees of the Estate of C. S. Lewis, renewed 1979 by Arthur Owen Barfield; *The Silver Chair*, Copyright 1953 by The Trustees of the Estate of C. S. Lewis, renewed 1981 by Arthur Owen Barfield; *The Voyage of the Dawn Treader*, Copyright 1952 by The Trustees of the Estate of C. S. Lewis, renewed 1980 by Arthur Owen Barfield; *The Great Divorce*, Copyright 1946 by Macmillan Publishing Co., Inc., renewed 1974 by Arthur Owen Barfield and Alfred Cecil Harwood; *The Lion, the Witch and the Wardrobe*, Copyright 1950 by The Trustees of the Estate of C. S. Lewis, renewed 1978 by Arthur Owen Barfield; *The Screwtape Letters*, Copyright C. S. Lewis 1942.
The Bodley Head, for excerpts from C. S. Lewis, *The Last Battle*, © 1956 by C. S. Lewis; *The Magician's Nephew*, Copyright 1955 by C. S. Lewis; *Out of the Silent Planet*, Macmillan Paperback Edition 1965; *Perelandra*, Copyright 1944 by Clive Staples Lewis, renewed 1972 by Arthur Owen Barfield and Alfred Cecil Harwood; *That Hideous Strength*, Copyright 1946 by Clive Staples Lewis, renewed 1974 by Arthur Owen Barfield and Alfred Cecil Harwood.

Macmillan Publishing Company
866 Third Avenue, New York, N.Y. 10022
Collier Macmillan Canada, Inc.

Library of Congress Cataloging in Publication Data

Lewis, C. S. (Clive Staples), 1898–1963.
    The visionary Christian.

    Bibliography: p.
    1. Theology—Addresses, essays, lectures.
1. Walsh, Chad, 1914–   II. Title.
BR85.L4846   1981   230   81-11770
ISBN 0-02-086730-1   AACR2

---

10   9   8   7   6   5   4   3

Printed in the United States of America

FOR

Frederick and Ercell Kullberg

Contents

Preface

IN LATE 1963 an assassin's bullet struck down the president of the United States. For days afterward, TV screens were dominated by the horror of the event, and the American public had time only for this one grief. It was as though the world had turned into a madman's nightmare.

Less strident events were taking place during the same period of time, but few of them found their way into the media. It was not until several days after the death of John Kennedy that I learned of two other deaths on the same day: Aldous Huxley, who with a massive overdose of psychedelic drugs evaded death by cancer, and C. S. Lewis, who departed quietly in consequence of a heart attack. I found myself remembering times I had been with him, in particular the last time, two years before his death. He was already seriously ill at that point with a combination of heart and kidney ailments, and he was subdued and lacking the verbal and intellectual fire I had come to associate with him.

My memories strayed to earlier occasions when I had seen him in robust health, eager to talk of religion and literature, still more eager to engage in debate, whether in a little group of friends, a public confrontation, or via the printed page. As the shock of his death wore off, I found myself asking the inevitable question: What will his reputation be ten years from now? Fifty years from now? Most writers sink at least partially out of sight when they are no longer visible, and for many of them there is no literary resurrection.

Well, an interim report is now possible. Lewis died almost two decades ago, and in America at least the public's interest in his work is at an all-time high. This is reflected in the phenomenal sale of his books, especially *Mere Christianity* and the seven Narnia chronicles. C. S. Lewis societies have sprung up, and a growing number of scholars are busy doing theological analyses of his books, or subjecting them to the specialized approaches of formal literary criticism. Meanwhile, many quite ordinary people (and some not so ordinary) have found in his writings a new understanding of Christianity. Many lives have been radically altered. It begins to appear that C. S. Lewis is an almost unique writer, in his ability to speak to all sorts and conditions, from the children reading a Narnia story to the professor of philosophy examining his use of Platonic concepts.

I can explain Lewis's appeal to such a diversity of readers only by seeing in him a writer who, to a very unusual degree, combined two sensibilities. Lewis number 1 was the logician, ruthless in debate with his adversaries, but equally strict with himself. He strove to avoid nonsense and faulty reasoning as though his soul were at stake, as he doubtless assumed it was. In such books as *Mere Christian-*

ity, The Problem of Pain, and *Miracles* he reveals this lobe of his brain at work.

The other lobe, Lewis number 2—the dreamer, the fantasizer, the superb creator of imagined worlds—is always hovering in the background but must yield priority to the logician. Perhaps more tellingly than any other widely read apologist of our times, he presents and defends the fundamental beliefs of Christianity. At the very least he leads the reader to the point where he sees no intellectual dishonesty in recognizing a live option in the ancient faith.

But if this were all, his public would be smaller and less dedicated. He might seem in retrospect a latter-day G. K. Chesterton, but not a writer whose books would inspire a veritable Lewis cult. To understand that, we must take into account the second lobe of his brain, where one of the most powerful literary imaginations of our century found ways to bring Christianity alive, not as a coolly rational system of thought and behavior, but as a way of looking at the cosmos and seeing its Creator at the center. By means of children's fairy tales, allegories, dream visions, poems, and science fiction, he brings Christianity alive and gleaming with promise. He takes the old legend of Cupid and Psyche and transforms it into *Till We Have Faces,* a tale with haunting emotional depth and a probing exploration of the human soul. Apart from Tolkien's books, it is hard to find any contemporary parallel to these achievements. The reader explores a universe in which mythology ever hints at realities beyond the drab common sense of our usual days.

It is the combination of the two Lewises that makes his accomplishments so powerful and haunting. One reader may prefer one aspect of Lewis and one another, but exposure to Lewis 1 has a way of leading to Lewis 2, and vice versa, until the total Lewis is reached.

The role of Christianity in Lewis's books varies with the literary genre in which he is writing. In his directly apologetic books, such as *Mere Christianity,* he zeros in on his target. He is out to expound and, if possible, convince. In the more imaginative books the theological presuppositions of the Christian faith are indeed always present also, sometimes explicitly, as in *The Lion, the Witch and the Wardrobe,* sometimes introduced gradually and more obliquely, as in *Out of the Silent Planet.*

It is a glowing and glorious universe that Lewis presents in his fantasies. It is at the same time a dangerous one. The forces of evil are locked in combat with the servants of God. However humble our status in this world, we are summoned to fight on one side or the other. Trusting that God is with us, we need not quail before the demonic powers, such as those embodied in the mad scientist, Weston, of the space trilogy, or the witch in the Narnia tales.

A few years ago William Griffin had the happy idea of assembling an anthology from Lewis's writings, entitled *The Joyful Christian.* In his book more than a hundred selections are collected between one set of covers. They deal with such themes as Life on Other Planets, Heaven, Hell, Atheism, Right and Wrong, Sex, and Marriage. The scope of Lewis's thought and the beliefs he held are powerfully presented in his own words.

The Joyful Christian is confined to Lewis's expository and apologetic religious books. It deliberately excludes the fantasies, except that Screwtape manages to sneak in. It represents Lewis 1 and dramatizes the power and profundity of his rational mind. But it occurred to me that a companion book is needed to bring together selections from his more fanciful works. I soon found that these books deal with the same major themes as those found in *The Joyful Christian.* I set about putting together the present book, *The Visionary Christian,* so that the reader can see the second Lewis at work. In the earlier anthology, one finds a straightforward doctrine of marriage, and in the present book he sees it dramatized through the growth in understanding of Jane Studdock, or the comments of that close observer of the human animal, Screwtape. Thus the two books deal with much the same topics, but in very different ways.

The Visionary Christian is a candid invitation to revel in the many imagined worlds of Lewis's vision, and to find in them the same preoccupation with major themes of spiritual life and death that dominate his apologetic books. Some doctrines that might seem prosaic in Mere Christianity may glow with a radiance not ordinarily seen on this earth, and inspire dreams of a universe in which there is always more to see than we as yet quite have the eyes to see.

In the trilogy we explore life on the planets Mars and Venus; in The Great Divorce we take a bus from hell (or is it purgatory?) to heaven; we share in the struggle against demonic principalities in That Hideous Strength; we watch Aslan creating Narnia, and we see that world brought to an end and replaced by the new Narnia.

Yet though we roam far in God's universe as envisioned by C. S. Lewis, all our adventures serve to bring us greater understanding of the here and now, on fallen Tellus. It is here, after all, that almost two thousand years ago God carried out his greatest counterattack against the demonic forces. By journeying, thanks to Lewis's imagination, to distant worlds, we see our own more clearly and are summoned to take our part in the ultimate defeat of the bent eldil. Lewis is never more relevant to our usual days and dreams and nightmares than when he guides us through the worlds he has created. My hope is that The Visionary Christian will help us to enjoy and understand the lands to which he so skilfully escorts us. One thing I can promise. We shall not be bored.

CHAD WALSH

March 1981

Normality

THE ROOM, at first sight, was an anticlimax. It appeared to be an empty committee room with a long table, eight or nine chairs, some pictures, and (oddly enough) a large stepladder in one corner. Here also there were no windows; it was lit by an electric light which produced, better than Mark had ever seen it produced before, the illusion of daylight—of a cold, grey place out of doors. This, combined with the absence of a fireplace, made it seem chilly though the temperature was not in fact very low.

A man of trained sensibility would have seen at once that the room was ill-proportioned, not grotesquely so, but sufficiently to produce dislike. It was too high and too narrow. Mark felt the effect without analysing the cause, and the effect grew on him as time passed. Sitting staring about him he next noticed the door—and thought at first that he

1

was the victim of some optical illusion. It took him quite a long time to prove to himself that he was not. The point of the arch was not in the centre: the whole thing was lopsided. Once again, the error was not gross. The thing was near enough to the true to deceive you for a moment and to go on teasing the mind even after the deception had been unmasked. Involuntarily one kept shifting the head to find positions from which it would look right after all. He turned round and sat with his back to it . . . one mustn't let it become an obsession.

Then he noticed the spots on the ceiling. They were not mere specks of dirt or discolouration. They were deliberately painted on: little round black spots placed at irregular intervals on the pale mustard-coloured surface. There were not a great many of them: perhaps thirty . . . or was it a hundred? He determined that he would not fall into the trap of trying to count them. They would be hard to count, they were so irregularly placed. Or weren't they? Now that his eyes were growing used to them (and one couldn't help noticing that there were five in that little group to the right), their arrangement seemed to hover on the verge of regularity. They suggested some kind of pattern. Their peculiar ugliness consisted in the very fact that they kept on suggesting it and then frustrating the expectation thus aroused. Suddenly he realised that this was another trap. He fixed his eyes on the table.

There were spots on the table too: white ones. Shiny white spots, not quite round. And arranged, apparently, to correspond to the spots on the ceiling. Or were they? No, of course not . . . ah, now he had it! The pattern (if you could call it a pattern) on the table was an exact reversal of that on the ceiling. But with certain exceptions. He found he was glancing rapidly from one to the other, trying to puzzle it out. For the third time he checked himself. He got up and began to walk about. He had a look at the pictures.

Some of them belonged to a school of art with which he

was already familiar. There was a portrait of a young woman who held her mouth wide open to reveal the fact that the inside of it was thickly overgrown with hair. It was very skilfully painted in the photographic manner so that you could almost feel that hair; indeed you could not avoid feeling it however hard you tried. There was a giant mantis playing a fiddle while being eaten by another mantis, and a man with corkscrews instead of arms bathing in a flat, sadly coloured sea beneath a summer sunset. But most of the pictures were not of this kind. At first, most of them seemed rather ordinary, though Mark was a little surprised at the predominance of scriptural themes. It was only at the second or third glance that one discovered certain unaccountable details—something odd about the positions of the figures' feet or the arrangement of their fingers or the grouping. And who was the person standing between the Christ and the Lazarus? And why were there so many beetles under the table in the Last Supper? What was the curious trick of lighting that made each picture look like something seen in delirium? When once these questions had been raised the apparent ordinariness of the pictures became their supreme menace—like the ominous surface innocence at the beginning of certain dreams. Every fold of drapery, every piece of architecture, had a meaning one could not grasp but which withered the mind. Compared with these the other, surrealistic, pictures were mere foolery. Long ago Mark had read somewhere of "things of that extreme evil which seem innocent to the uninitiate," and had wondered what sort of things they might be. Now he felt he knew.

He turned his back on the pictures and sat down. He understood the whole business now. Frost was not trying to make him insane; at least not in the sense Mark had hitherto given to the word "insanity." Frost had meant what he said. To sit in the room was the first step towards what Frost called objectivity—the process whereby all specifically human reactions were killed in a man so that he might become fit for the fastidious society of the Macrobes. Higher degrees in the asceticism of anti-Nature would doubtless follow: the eating of abominable food, the dabbling in dirt and blood, the ritual performances of calculated obscenities. They were, in a sense, playing quite fair with him—offering him the very same initiation through which they themselves had passed and which had divided them from humanity, distending and dissipating Wither into a shapeless ruin while it condensed and sharpened Frost into the hard, bright, little needle that he now was.

But after an hour or so this long, high coffin of a room began to produce on Mark an effect which his instructor had probably not anticipated. There was no return of the attack which he had suffered last night in the cell. Whether because he had already survived that attack, or because the imminence of death had drawn the tooth of his lifelong desire for the esoteric, or because he had (in a fashion) called very urgently for help, the built and painted perversity of this room had the effect of making him aware, as he had never been aware before, of this room's opposite. As the desert first teaches men to love water, or as absence first reveals affection, there rose up against this background of the sour and the crooked some kind of vision of the sweet and the straight. Something else—something he vaguely called the "Normal"—apparently existed. He had never thought about it before. But there it was—solid, massive, with a shape of its own, almost like something you could touch, or eat, or fall in love with. It was all mixed up with Jane and fried eggs and soap and sunlight and the rooks cawing at Cure Hardy and the thought that, somewhere outside, daylight was going on at that moment. He was not thinking in moral terms at all; or else (what is much the same thing) he was having his first deeply moral experience. He was choosing a side: the Normal. "All that," as he called it, was what he chose. If the scientific point of view led away from "all that," then be damned to the scientific point of view! The vehemence of his choice almost took his breath away; he had not had such a sensation before. For the moment he hardly cared if Frost and Wither killed him.

Ordinary People

IN PRAISE OF SOLID PEOPLE

Thank God that there are solid folk
Who water flowers and roll the lawn,
And sit and sew and talk and smoke,
And snore all through the summer dawn.

Who pass untroubled nights and days
Full-fed and sleepily content,
Rejoicing in each other's praise,
Respectable and innocent.

Who feel the things that all men feel,
And think in well-worn grooves of thought,
Whose honest spirits never reel
Before man's mystery, overwrought.

Yet not unfaithful nor unkind,
With work-day virtues surely staid,
Theirs is the sane and humble mind,
And full affections undismayed.

O happy people! I have seen
No verse yet written in your praise,
And, truth to tell, the time has been
I would have scorned your easy ways.

But now thro' weariness and strife
I learn your worthiness indeed,
The world is better for such life
As stout, suburban people lead.

Too often have I sat alone
When the wet night falls heavily,
And fretting winds around me moan,
And homeless longing vexes me

For lore that I shall never know,
And visions none can hope to see,
Till brooding works upon me so
A childish fear steals over me.

I look around the empty room,
The clock still ticking in its place,
And all else silent as the tomb,
Till suddenly, I think, a face

Grows from the darkness just beside.
I turn, and lo! it fades away,
And soon another phantom tide
Of shifting dreams begins to play,

And dusky galleys past me sail,
Full freighted on a faerie sea;
I hear the silken merchants hail
Across the ringing waves to me

—Then suddenly, again, the room,
Familiar books about me piled,
And I alone amid the gloom,
By one more mocking dream beguiled.

And still no nearer to the Light,
And still no further from myself,
Alone and lost in clinging night
—(The clock's still ticking on the shelf).

Then do I envy solid folk
Who sit of evenings by the fire,
After their work and doze and smoke,
And are not fretted by desire.

The Crooked and the Straight

MEANWHILE, in the Objective Room, something like a crisis
had developed between Mark and Professor Frost. As soon
as they arrived there Mark saw that the table had been
drawn back. On the floor lay a large crucifix, almost life
size, a work of art in the Spanish tradition, ghastly and realistic. "We have half an hour to pursue our exercises," said
Frost looking at his watch. Then he instructed Mark to
trample on it and insult it in other ways.

Now whereas Jane had abandoned Christianity in early
childhood, along with her belief in fairies and Santa Claus,
Mark had never believed in it at all. At this moment, therefore, it crossed his mind for the very first time that there
might conceivably be something in it. Frost, who was
watching him carefully, knew perfectly well that this might
be the result of the present experiment. He knew it for the
very good reason that his own training by the Macrobes
had, at one point, suggested the same odd idea to himself.
But he had no choice. Whether he wished it or not this sort
of thing was part of the initiation.

"But, look here," said Mark.

"What is it?" said Frost. "Pray be quick. We have only a
limited time at our disposal."

"This," said Mark, pointing with an undefined reluctance
to the horrible white figure on the cross. "This is all surely
a pure superstition."

"Well?"

"Well, if so, what is there objective about stamping on the face? Isn't it just as subjective to spit on a thing like this as to worship it? I mean—damn it all—if it's only a bit of wood, why do anything about it?"

"That is superficial. If you had been brought up in a non-Christian society, you would not be asked to do this. Of course, it is a superstition; but it is that particular superstition which has pressed upon our society for a great many centuries. It can be experimentally shown that it still forms a dominant system in the subconscious of many individuals whose conscious thought appears to be wholly liberated. An explicit action in the reverse direction is therefore a necessary step towards complete objectivity. It is not a question for *a priori* discussion. We find it in practice that it cannot be dispensed with."

Mark himself was surprised at the emotions he was undergoing. He did not regard the image with anything at all like a religious feeling. Most emphatically it did not belong to that idea of the Straight or Normal or Wholesome which had, for the last few days, been his support against what he now knew of the innermost circle at Belbury. The horrible vigour of its realism was, indeed, in its own way as remote from that Idea as anything else in the room. That was one source of his reluctance. To insult even a carved image of such agony seemed an abominable act. But it was not the only source. With the introduction of this Christian symbol the whole situation had somehow altered. The thing was becoming incalculable. His simple antithesis of the Normal and the Diseased had obviously failed to take something into account. Why was the crucifix there? Why were more than half the poison-pictures religious? He had the sense of new parties to the conflict—potential allies and enemies which he had not suspected before. "If I take a step in any direction," he thought, "I may step over a precipice." A donkey-like determination to plant hoofs and stay still at all costs arose in his mind.

"Pray make haste," said Frost.

The quiet urgency of the voice, and the fact that he had so often obeyed it before, almost conquered him. He was on the verge of obeying, and getting the whole silly business over, when the defencelessness of the figure deterred him. The feeling was a very illogical one. Not because its hands were nailed and helpless, but because they were only made of wood and therefore even more helpless, because the thing, for all its realism, was inanimate and could not in any way hit back, he paused. The unretaliating face of a doll—one of Myrtle's dolls—which he had pulled to pieces in boyhood had affected him in the same way and the memory, even now, was tender to the touch.

"What are you waiting for, Mr. Studdock?" said Frost.

Mark was well aware of the rising danger. Obviously, if he disobeyed, his last chance of getting out of Belbury alive might be gone. Even of getting out of this room. The smothering sensation once again attacked him. He was himself, he felt, as helpless as the wooden Christ. As he thought this, he found himself looking at the crucifix in a new way—neither as a piece of wood nor a monument of superstition but as a bit of history. Christianity was nonsense, but one did not doubt that the man had lived and had been executed thus by the Belbury of those days. And that, as he suddenly saw, explained why this image, though not itself an image of the Straight or Normal, was yet in opposition to crooked Belbury. It was a picture of what happened when the Straight met the Crooked, a picture of what the Crooked did to the Straight—what it would do to him if he remained straight. It was, in a more emphatic sense than he had yet understood, a *cross*.

The Experience of "Joy"

HOWEVER, HE WENT ON always a few yards further till suddenly he looked up and saw that he was so far away from home that he was in a part of the road he had never seen before. Then came the sound of a musical instrument, from behind it seemed, very sweet and very short, as if it were one plucking of a string or one note of a bell, and after it a full, clear voice—and it sounded so high and strange that he thought it was very far away, further than a star. The voice said, Come. Then John saw that there was a stone wall beside the road in that part: but it had (what he had never seen in a garden wall before) a window. There was no glass in the window and no bars; it was just a square hole in the wall. Through it he saw a green wood full of primroses: and he remembered suddenly how he had gone into another wood to pull primroses, as a child, very long ago—so long that even in the moment of remembering the memory seemed still out of reach. While he strained to grasp it, there came to him from beyond the wood a sweetness and a pang so piercing that instantly he forgot his father's house, and his mother, and the fear of the Landlord, and the burden of the rules. All the furniture of his mind was taken away. A moment later he found that he was sobbing, and the sun had gone in: and what it was that had happened to him he could not quite remember, nor whether it had happened in this wood, or in the other wood when he was a child. It seemed to him that a mist which hung at the far end of the wood had parted for a moment, and through the rift he had seen a calm sea, and in the sea an island, where the smooth turf sloped down unbroken to the bays, and out of the thickets peeped the pale, small-breasted Oreads, wise like gods, unconscious of themselves like beasts, and tall enchanters, bearded to their feet, sat in green chairs among the forests. But even while he pictured these things he knew, with one part of his mind, that they were not like the things he had seen—nay, that what had befallen him was not seeing at all. But he was too young to heed the distinction: and too empty, now that the unbounded sweetness passed away, not to seize greedily whatever it had left behind. He had no inclination yet to go into the wood: and presently he went home, with a sad excitement upon him, repeating to himself a thousand times, "I know now what I want."

The Quest

PROLOGUE

As of old Phoenician men, to the Tin Isles sailing
Straight against the sunset and the edges of the earth,
Chaunted loud above the storm and the strange sea's
    wailing,
Legends of their people and the land that gave them
    birth—
Sang aloud to Baal-Peor, sang unto the horned maiden,
Sang how they should come again with the Brethon treasure
    laden,
Sang of all the pride and glory of their hardy enterprise,
How they found the outer islands, where the unknown
    stars arise;
And the rowers down below, rowing hard as they could
    row,
Toiling at the stroke and feather through the wet and weary
    weather,
Even they forgot their burden in the measure of a song,
And the merchants and the masters and the bondmen all
    together,
Dreaming of the wondrous islands, brought the gallant ship
    along;
So in mighty deeps alone on the chainless breezes blown
In my coracle of verses I will sing of lands unknown,
Flying from the scarlet city where a Lord that knows no pity
Mocks the broken people praying round his iron throne,
—Sing about the Hidden Country fresh and full of quiet
    green.
Sailing over seas uncharted to a port that none has seen.

Purgatory and / or Hell

I SEEMED TO BE STANDING in a bus queue by the side of a long, mean street. Evening was just closing in and it was raining. I had been wandering for hours in similar mean streets, always in the rain and always in evening twilight. Time seemed to have paused on that dismal moment when only a few shops have lit up and it is not yet dark enough for their windows to look cheering. And just as the evening never advanced to night, so my walking had never brought me to the better parts of the town. However far I went I found only dingy lodging houses, small tobacconists, hoardings from which posters hung in rags, windowless warehouses, goods stations without trains, and bookshops of the sort that sell *The Works of Aristotle*. I never met anyone. But for the little crowd at the bus stop, the whole town seemed to be empty. I think that was why I attached myself to the queue.

I had a stroke of luck right away, for just as I took my stand a little waspish woman who would have been ahead of me snapped out at a man who seemed to be with her, "Very well, then. I won't go at all. So there," and left the queue. "Pray don't imagine," said the man, in a very dignified voice, "that I care about going in the least. I have only been trying to please *you*, for peace sake. My own feelings are of course a matter of no importance. I quite understand *that*"—and suiting the action to the word he also walked away. "Come," thought I, "that's two places gained." I was now next to a very short man with a scowl who glanced at me with an expression of extreme disfavour and observed, rather unnecessarily loudly, to the man beyond him, "This sort of thing really makes one think twice about going at all." "What sort of thing?" growled the other, a big beefy person. "Well," said the Short Man, "this is hardly the sort of society I'm used to as a matter of fact." "Huh!" said the Big Man: and then added with a glance at me, "Don't you stand any sauce from *him*, Mister. You're not *afraid* of him, are you?" Then, seeing I made no move, he rounded suddenly on the Short Man and said, "Not good enough for you, aren't we? Like your lip." Next moment he had fetched the Short Man one on the side of the face that sent him sprawling into the gutter. "Let him lay, let him lay," said the Big Man to no-one in particular. "I'm a plain man that's what I am and I got to have my rights same as anyone else, see?" As the Short Man showed no disposition to rejoin the queue and soon began limping away, I closed up, rather cautiously, behind the Big Man and congratulated myself on having gained yet another step. A moment later two young people in front of him also left us arm in arm. They were both so trousered, slender, giggly and falsetto that I could be sure of the sex of neither, but it was clear that each for the moment preferred the other to the chance of a place in the bus. "We shall never all get in," said a female voice with a whine in it from some four places ahead of me. "Change places with you for five bob, lady," said someone else. I heard the clink of money and then a scream in the female voice, mixed with roars of laughter from the rest of the crowd. The cheated woman leaped out of her place to fly at the man who had bilked her, but the other immediately closed up and flung her out. . . . So what with one thing and another the queue had reduced itself to manageable proportions long before the bus appeared.

Passengers on the Heavenly Bus

IT WAS A WONDERFUL VEHICLE, blazing with golden light, heraldically coloured. The Driver himself seemed full of light and he used only one hand to drive with. The other he waved before his face as if to fan away the greasy steam of the rain. A growl went up from the queue as he came in sight. "Looks as if *he* had a good time of it, eh? . . . Bloody pleased with himself, I bet. . . . My dear, why can't he behave *naturally?*—Thinks himself too good to look at us. . . . Who does he imagine he is? . . . All that gilding and purple, I call it a wicked waste. Why don't they spend some of the money on their house property down here?—God! I'd like to give him one in the ear-'ole." I could see nothing in the countenance of the Driver to justify all this, unless it were that he had a look of authority and seemed intent on carrying out his job.

My fellow passengers fought like hens to get on board the bus though there was plenty of room for us all. I was the last to get in. The bus was only half full and I selected a seat at the back, well away from the others. But a tousle-headed youth at once came and sat down beside me. As he did so we moved off.

"I thought you wouldn't mind my tacking on to you," he said, "for I've noticed that you feel just as I do about the present company. Why on earth they insist on coming I can't imagine. They won't like it at all when we get there, and they'd really be much more comfortable at home. It's different for you and me."

"Do they *like* this place?" I asked.

"As much as they'd like anything," he answered.

"They've got cinemas and fish and chip shops and advertisements and all the sorts of things they want. The appalling lack of any intellectual life doesn't worry *them*. I realised as soon as I got here that there'd been some mistake. I ought to have taken the first bus but I've fooled about trying to wake people up here. I found a few fellows I'd known before and tried to form a little circle, but they all seem to have sunk to the level of their surroundings. Even before we came here I'd had some doubts about a man like Cyril Blellow. I always thought he was working in a false idiom. But he was at least intelligent: one could get some criticism worth hearing from him, even if he was a failure on the creative side. But now he seems to have nothing left but his self-conceit. The last time I tried to read him some of my own stuff . . . but wait a minute, I'd just like you to look at it."

Realising with a shudder that what he was producing from his pocket was a thick wad of typewritten paper, I muttered something about not having my spectacles and exclaimed, "Hullo! We've left the ground."

It was true. Several hundred feet below us, already half hidden in the rain and mist, the wet roofs of the town appeared, spreading without a break as far as the eye could reach.

At the Border of Heaven

HOURS LATER there came a change. It began to grow light in the bus. The greyness outside the windows turned from mud-colour to mother of pearl, then to faintest blue, then to a bright blueness that stung the eyes. We seemed to be floating in a pure vacancy. There were no lands, no sun, no stars in sight: only the radiant abyss. I let down the window beside me. Delicious freshness came in for a second, and then—

"What the hell are you doing?" shouted the Intelligent Man, leaning roughly across me and pulling the window sharply up. "Want us all to catch our death of cold?"

"Hit him a biff," said the Big Man.

I glanced round the bus. Though the windows were closed, and soon muffed, the bus was full of light. It was cruel light. I shrank from the faces and forms by which I was surrounded. They were all fixed faces, full not of possibilities but of impossibilities, some gaunt, some bloated, some glaring with idiotic ferocity, some drowned beyond recovery in dreams; but all, in one way or another, distorted and faded. One had a feeling that they might fall to pieces at any moment if the light grew much stronger. Then—there was a mirror on the end wall of the bus—I caught sight of my own.

And still the light grew.

A CLIFF had loomed up ahead. It sank vertically beneath us so far that I could not see the bottom, and it was dark and smooth. We were mounting all the time. At last the top of the cliff became visible like a thin line of emerald green stretched tight as a fiddle-string. Presently we glided over that top: we were flying above a level, grassy country through which there ran a wide river. We were losing height now: some of the tallest tree tops were only twenty feet below us. Then, suddenly we were at rest. Everyone had jumped up. Curses, taunts, blows, a filth of vituperation, came to my ears as my fellow-passengers struggled to get out. A moment later, and they had all succeeded. I was alone in the bus, and through the open door there came to me in the fresh stillness the singing of a lark.

I got out. The light and coolness that drenched me were like those of summer morning, early morning a minute or

two before the sunrise, only that there was a certain difference. I had the sense of being in a larger space, perhaps
even a larger *sort* of space, than I had ever known before: as
if the sky were further off and the extent of the green plain
wider than they could be on this little ball of earth. I had
got "out" in some sense which made the Solar System itself
seem an indoor affair. It gave me a feeling of freedom, but
also of exposure, possibly of danger, which continued to
accompany me through all that followed. It is the impossi-
bility of communicating that feeling, or even of inducing
you to remember it as I proceed, which makes me despair
of conveying the real quality of what I saw and heard.

At first, of course, my attention was caught by my fellow-
passengers, who were still grouped about in the neighbourhood of the omnibus, though beginning, some of them, to
walk forward into the landscape with hesitating steps. I
gasped when I saw them. Now that they were in the light,
they were transparent—fully transparent when they stood
between me and it, smudgy and imperfectly opaque when
they stood in the shadow of some tree. They were in fact
ghosts: man-shaped stains on the brightness of that air.
One could attend to them or ignore them at will as you do
with the dirt on a window pane. I noticed that the grass did
not bend under their feet: even the dew drops were not
disturbed.

Then some re-adjustment of the mind or some focussing
of my eyes took place, and I saw the whole phenomenon
the other way round. The men were as they always had
been; as all the men I had known had been perhaps. It was
the light, the grass, the trees that were different; made of
some different substance, so much solider than things in
our country that men were ghosts by comparison. Moved
by a sudden thought, I bent down and tried to pluck a daisy
which was growing at my feet. The stalk wouldn't break. I
tried to twist it, but it wouldn't twist. I tugged till the sweat
stood out on my forehead and I had lost most of the skin off

my hands. The little flower was hard, not like wood or even like iron, but like diamond. There was a leaf—a young tender beech-leaf, lying in the grass beside it. I tried to pick the leaf up: my heart almost cracked with the effort, and I believe I did just raise it. But I had to let it go at once; it was heavier than a sack of coal. As I stood, recovering my breath with great gasps and looking down at the daisy, I noticed that I could see the grass not only between my feet but *through* them. I also was a phantom. Who will give me words to express the terror of that discovery? "Golly!" thought I. "I'm in for it this time."

The Double Ghost

WHILE WE SPOKE the Lady was steadily advancing towards us, but it was not at us she looked. Following the direction of her eyes, I turned and saw an oddly shaped phantom approaching. Or rather two phantoms: a great tall Ghost, horribly thin and shaky, who seemed to be leading on a chain another Ghost no bigger than an organ-grinder's monkey. The taller Ghost wore a soft black hat, and he reminded me of something that my memory could not quite recover. Then, when he had come within a few feet of the Lady he spread out his lean, shaky hand flat on his chest with the fingers wide apart, and exclaimed in a hollow voice, "At last!" All at once I realised what it was that he had put me in mind of. He was like a seedy actor of the old school.

"Darling! At last!" said the Lady. "Good Heavens!" thought I. "Surely she can't——," and then I noticed two things. In the first place, I noticed that the little Ghost was not being led by the big one. It was the dwarfish figure that held the chain in its hand and the theatrical figure that wore the collar round its neck. In the second place, I noticed that the Lady was looking solely at the dwarf Ghost. She seemed to think it was the Dwarf who had addressed her, or else she was deliberately ignoring the other. On the poor dwarf she turned her eyes. Love shone not from her face only, but from all her limbs, as if it were some liquid in which she had just been bathing. Then, to my dismay she came nearer. She stooped down and kissed the Dwarf. It made one shudder to see her in such close contact with that cold, damp, shrunken thing. But she did not shudder.

"Frank," she said, "before anything else, forgive me. For all I ever did wrong and for all I did not do right since the first day we met, I ask your pardon."

I looked properly at the Dwarf for the first time now: or perhaps, when he received her kiss he became a little more visible. One could just make out the sort of face he must have had when he was a man: a little, oval, freckled face with a weak chin and a tiny wisp of unsuccessful moustache. He gave her a glance, not a full look. He was watching the Tragedian out of the corner of his eyes. Then he gave a jerk to the chain: and it was the Tragedian, not he, who answered the Lady.

"There, there," said the Tragedian. "We'll say no more about it. We all make mistakes." With the words there came over his features a ghastly contortion which, I think, was meant for an indulgently playful smile. "We'll say no more," he continued. "It's not myself I'm thinking about. It is you. That is what has been continually on my mind—all these years. The thought of you—you here alone, breaking your heart about me."

"But now," said the Lady to the Dwarf, "you can set all that aside. Never think like that again. It is all over."

Her beauty brightened so that I could hardly see anything else, and under that sweet compulsion the Dwarf really looked at her for the first time. For a second I thought he was growing more like a man. He opened his mouth. He himself was going to speak this time. But oh, the disappointment when the words came!

"You missed me?" he croaked in a small, bleating voice.

Yet even then she was not taken aback. Still the love and courtesy flowed from her.

"Dear, you will understand about that very soon," she said. "But to-day——."

What happened next gave me a shock. The Dwarf and the Tragedian spoke in unison, not to her but to one another. "You'll notice," they warned one another, "she hasn't answered our question." I realised then that they were one person, or rather that both were the remains of what had once been a person. The Dwarf again rattled the chain.

"You missed me?" said the Tragedian to the Lady, throwing a dreadful theatrical tremor into his voice.

"Dear friend," said the Lady, still attending exclusively to the Dwarf, "you may be happy about that and about everything else. Forget all about it for ever."

And really, for a moment, I thought the Dwarf was going to obey: partly because the outlines of his face became a little clearer, and partly because the invitation to all joy, singing out of her whole being like a bird's song on an April evening, seemed to me such that no creature could resist it. Then he hesitated. And then—once more he and his accomplice spoke in unison.

"Of course it would be rather fine and magnanimous not to press the point," they said to one another. "But can we be sure she'd notice? We've done these sorts of things before. There was the time we let her have the last stamp in the house to write to her mother and said nothing although she *had* known we wanted to write a letter ourself. We'd thought she'd remember and see how unselfish we'd been. But she never did. And there was the time . . . oh, lots and lots of times!" So the Dwarf gave a shake to the chain and—.

"I can't forget it," cried the Tragedian. "And I won't forget it, either. I could forgive them all they've done to me. But for your miseries—."

"Oh, don't you understand?" said the Lady. "There *are* no miseries here."

"Do you mean to say," answered the Dwarf, as if this new idea had made him quite forget the Tragedian for a moment, "do you mean to say you've been *happy?*"

"Didn't you want me to be? But no matter. Want it now. Or don't think about it at all."

The Dwarf blinked at her. One could see an unheard-of idea trying to enter his little mind: one could see even that there was for him some sweetness in it. For a second he had almost let the chain go: then, as if it were his life-line, he clutched it once more.

The Heavens of Space

THE PERIOD SPENT IN THE SPACE-SHIP ought to have been one of terror and anxiety for Ransom. He was separated by an astronomical distance from every member of the human race except two whom he had excellent reasons for distrusting. He was heading for an unknown destination, and was being brought thither for a purpose which his captors steadily refused to disclose. Devine and Weston relieved each other regularly in a room which Ransom was never allowed to enter and where he supposed the controls of their machine must be. Weston, during his watches off, was almost entirely silent. Devine was more loquacious and would often talk and guffaw with the prisoner until Weston rapped on the wall of the control-room and warned them not to waste air. But Devine was secretive after a certain point. He was quite ready to laugh at Weston's solemn scientific idealism. He didn't give a damn, he said, for the future of the species or the meeting of two worlds.

"There's more to Malacandra than that," he would add with a wink. But when Ransom asked him what more, he would lapse into satire and make ironical remarks about the white man's burden and the blessings of civilization.

"It *is* inhabited, then?" Ransom would press.

"Ah—there's always a native question in these things," Devine would answer. For the most part his conversation ran on the things he would do when he got back to Earth: ocean-going yachts, the most expensive women and a big place on the Riviera figured largely in his plans. "I'm not running all these risks for fun."

Direct questions about Ransom's own role were usually met with silence. Only once, in reply to such a question, Devine, who was then in Ransom's opinion very far from sober, admitted that they were rather "handing him the baby."

"But I'm sure," he added, "you'll live up to the old school tie."

All this, as I have said, was sufficiently disquieting. The odd thing was that it did not very greatly disquiet him. It is hard for a man to brood on the future when he is feeling so extremely well as Ransom now felt. There was an endless night on one side of the ship and an endless day on the other: each was marvellous and he moved from the one to the other at his will, delighted. In the nights, which he could create by turning the handle of a door, he lay for hours in contemplation of the skylight. The Earth's disk was nowhere to be seen; the stars, thick as daisies on an uncut lawn, reigned perpetually with no cloud, no moon, no sunrise to dispute their sway. There were planets of unbelievable majesty, and constellations undreamed of: there were celestial sapphires, rubies, emeralds and pin-pricks of burning gold; far out on the left of the picture hung a comet, tiny and remote: and between all and behind all, far more emphatic and palpable than it showed on Earth, the undimensioned, enigmatic blackness. The lights trembled: they seemed to grow brighter as he looked. Stretched naked on his bed, a second Danaë, he found it night by night more difficult to disbelieve in old astrology: almost he felt, wholly he imagined, "sweet influence" pouring or even stabbing into his surrendered body. All was silence but for the irregular tinkling noises. He knew now that these were made by meteorites, small, drifting particles of the world-stuff that smote continually on their hollow drum of steel; and he guessed that at any moment they might meet something large enough to make meteorites of ship and all. But he could not fear. He now felt that Weston had justly called him little-minded in the moment of his first panic. The adventure was too high, its circumstance too solemn, for any emotion save a severe delight. But the days—that is, the hours spent in the sunward hemisphere of their microcosm—were the best of all. Often he rose after only a few hours' sleep to return, drawn by an irresistible attraction, to the regions of light; he could not cease to wonder at the noon which always awaited you however early you went to seek it. There, totally immersed in a bath of pure ethereal colour and of unrelenting though unwounding brightness, stretched his full length and with eyes half closed in the strange chariot that bore them, faintly quivering, through depth after depth of tranquillity far above the reach of night, he felt his body and mind daily rubbed and scoured and filled with new vitality. Weston, in one of his brief, reluctant answers, admitted a scientific basis for these sensations: they were receiving, he said, many rays that never penetrated the terrestrial atmosphere.

But Ransom, as time wore on, became aware of another and more spiritual cause for his progressive lightening and exultation of heart. A nightmare, long engendered in the modern mind by the mythology that follows in the wake of science, was falling off him. He had read of "Space": at the back of his thinking for years had lurked the dismal fancy of the black, cold vacuity, the utter deadness, which was supposed to separate the worlds. He had not known how much it affected him till now—now that the very name "Space" seemed a blasphemous libel for this empyrean ocean of radiance in which they swam. He could not call it "dead"; he felt life pouring into him from it every moment. How indeed should it be otherwise, since out of this ocean the worlds and all their life had come? He had thought it barren: he saw now that it was the womb of worlds, whose blazing and innumerable offspring looked down nightly even upon the earth with so many eyes—and here, with how many more! No: Space was the wrong name. Older thinkers had been wiser when they named it simply the heavens—the heavens which declared the glory—the

> happy climes that ly
> Where day never shuts his eye
> Up in the broad fields of the sky.

He quoted Milton's words to himself lovingly, at this time and often.

Prayer

FAR AWAY there appeared a red light. Then it disappeared for a moment and came back again, bigger and stronger. Then he could see dark shapes going to and fro on this side of the light and carrying bundles and throwing them down. He knew now what he was looking at. It was a bonfire, newly lit, and people were throwing bundles of brushwood onto it. Presently it blazed up and Tirian could see that it was on the very top of the hill. He could see quite clearly the stable behind it, all lit up in the red glow, and a great crowd of Beasts and Men between the fire and himself. A small figure, hunched up beside the fire, must be the Ape. It was saying something to the crowd, but he could not hear what. Then it went and bowed three times to the ground in front of the door of the stable. Then it got up and opened the door. And something on four legs—something that walked rather stiffly—came out of the stable and stood facing the crowd.

A great wailing or howling went up, so loud that Tirian could hear some of the words.

"Aslan! Aslan! Aslan!" cried the Beasts. "Speak to us. Comfort us. Be angry with us no more."

From where Tirian was, he could not make out very clearly what the thing was; but he could see that it was yellow and hairy. He had never seen the Great Lion. He had never seen a common lion. He couldn't be sure that what he saw was not the real Aslan. He had not expected Aslan to look like that stiff thing which stood and said nothing. But how could one be sure? For a moment horrible thoughts went through his mind: then he remembered the nonsense about Tash and Aslan being the same and knew that the whole thing must be a cheat.

The Ape put his head close up to the yellow thing's head as if he were listening to something it was whispering to him. Then he turned and spoke to the crowd, and the crowd wailed again. Then the yellow thing turned clumsily round and walked—you might almost say, waddled—back into the stable and the Ape shut the door behind it. After that the fire must have been put out for the light vanished quite suddenly, and Tirian was once more alone with the cold and the darkness.

He thought of other Kings who had lived and died in Narnia in old times and it seemed to him that none of them had ever been so unlucky as himself. He thought of his great-grandfather's great-grandfather, King Rilian, who had been stolen away by a Witch when he was only a young prince and kept hidden for years in the dark caves beneath the land of the Northern Giants. But then it had all come right in the end, for two mysterious children had suddenly appeared from the land beyond the world's end and had rescued him so that he came home to Narnia and had a long and prosperous reign. "It's not like that with me," said Tirian to himself. Then he went further back and thought about Rilian's father, Caspian the Seafarer, whose wicked uncle King Miraz had tried to murder him, and how Caspian fled away into the woods and lived among the Dwarfs. But that story had all come right in the end too: for Caspian also had been helped by children—only there were four of them that time—who came from somewhere beyond the world and fought a great battle and set him on his father's throne. "But it was all long ago," said Tirian to himself. "That sort of thing doesn't happen now." And then he remembered (for he had always been good at history when he was a boy) how those same four children who had helped Caspian had been in Narnia over a thousand years before; and it was then that they had defeated the terrible White Witch and ended the Hundred Years of Winter, and after that they had reigned (all four of them together) at Cair Paravel, till they were no longer children but great Kings and lovely Queens, and their reign had been the golden age of Narnia. And Aslan had come into that story a lot. He had come into all the other stories too, as Tirian now remembered. "Aslan—and children from another world," thought Tirian. "They have always come in when things were at their worst. Oh, if only they could now."

. And he called out "Aslan! Aslan! Aslan! Come and help us Now."

But the darkness and the cold and the quietness went on just the same.

"Let *me* be killed," cried the King. "I ask nothing for myself. But come and save all Narnia."

And still there was no change in the night or the wood, but there began to be a kind of change inside Tirian. Without knowing why, he began to feel a faint hope. And he felt somehow stronger. "Oh Aslan, Aslan," he whispered. "If you will not come yourself, at least send me the helpers from beyond the world. Or let me call them. Let my voice carry beyond the world." Then, hardly knowing that he was doing it, he suddenly cried out in a great voice:

"Children! Children! Friends of Narnia! Quick. Come to me. Across the worlds I call you; I Tirian, King of Narnia, Lord of Cair Paravel, and Emperor of the Lone Islands!"

A Prayer in Verse

THE APOLOGIST'S EVENING PRAYER

From all my lame defeats and oh! much more
From all the victories that I seemed to score;
From cleverness shot forth on Thy behalf
At which, while angels weep, the audience laugh;
From all my proofs of Thy divinity,
Thou, who wouldst give no sign, deliver me.

Thoughts are but coins. Let me not trust, instead
Of Thee, their thin-worn image of Thy head.
From all my thoughts, even from my thoughts of Thee,
O thou fair Silence, fall, and set me free.
Lord of the narrow gate and the needle's eye,
Take from me all my trumpery lest I die.

First Experience of Sex

WHEN HE LOOKED ROUND he saw what he had never expected, yet he was not surprised. There in the grass beside
him sat a laughing brown girl of about his own age, and
she had no clothes on.

"It was me you wanted," said the brown girl. "I am better than your silly Islands."

And John rose and caught her, all in haste, and committed fornication with her in the wood.

After that John was always going to the wood. He did not
always have his pleasure of her in the body, though it often

ended that way: sometimes he would talk to her about himself, telling her lies about his courage and his cleverness. All that he told her she remembered, so that on other days she could tell it over to him again. Sometimes, even, he would go with her through the wood looking for the sea and the Island, but not often. Meanwhile the year went on and the leaves began to fall in the wood and the skies were more often grey: until now, as I dreamed, John had slept in the wood, and he woke up in the wood. The sun was low and a blustering wind was stripping the leaves from the branches. The girl was still there and the appearance of her was hateful to John: and he saw that she knew this, and the more she knew it the more she stared at him, smiling. He looked round and saw how small the wood was after all—a beggarly strip of trees between the road and a field that he knew well. Nowhere in sight was there anything that he liked at all.

"I shall not come back here," said John. "What I wanted is not here. It wasn't you I wanted, you know."

"Wasn't it?" said the brown girl. "Then be off. But you must take your family with you."

With that she put up her hands to her mouth and called. Instantly from behind every tree there slipped out a brown girl: each of them was just like herself: the little wood was full of them.

"What are these?"

"Our daughters," said she. "Did you not know you were a father? Did you think I was barren, you fool? And now, children," she added, turning to the mob, "go with your father."

Suddenly John became very much afraid and leaped over the wall into the road. There he ran home as fast as he could.

Love

LOVE'S AS WARM AS TEARS

Love's as warm as tears,
        Love is tears:
Pressure within the brain,
Tension at the throat,
Deluge, weeks of rain,
Haystacks afloat,
Featureless seas between
Hedges, where once was green.

Love's as fierce as fire,
        Love is fire:
All sorts—infernal heat
Clinkered with greed and pride,
Lyric desire, sharp-sweet,
Laughing, even when denied,
And that empyreal flame
Whence all loves came.

Love's as fresh as spring,
        Love is spring:
Bird-song hung in the air,
Cool smells in a wood,
Whispering "Dare! Dare!"
To sap, to blood,
Telling "Ease, safety, rest,
Are good; not best."

Love's as hard as nails,
        Love is nails:

Blunt, thick, hammered through
The medial nerves of One
Who, having made us, knew
The thing He had done,
Seeing (what all that is)
Our cross, and His.

Love and Sex

"IS THE BEGETTING OF YOUNG not a pleasure among the *hrossa?*"

"A very great one, *Hmān.* This is what we call love."

"If a thing is a pleasure, a *hmān* wants it again. He might want the pleasure more often than the number of young that could be fed."

It took Hyoi a long time to get the point.

"You mean," he said slowly, "that he might do it not only in one or two years of his life but again?"

"Yes."

"But why? Would he want his dinner all day or want to sleep after he had slept? I do not understand."

"But a dinner comes every day. This love, you say, comes only once while the *hross* lives?"

"But it takes his whole life. When he is young he has to look for his mate; and then he has to court her; then he begets young; then he rears them; then he remembers all this, and boils it inside him and makes it into poems and wisdom."

"But the pleasure he must be content only to remember?"

"That is like saying 'My food I must be content to eat.' "

"I do not understand."

"A pleasure is full grown only when it is remembered. You are speaking, *Hmān,* as if the pleasure were one thing and the memory another. It is all one thing. The *séroni* could say it better than I say it now. Not better than I could say it in a poem. What you call remembering is the last part of the pleasure, as the *crah* is the last part of a poem. When you and I met, the meeting was over very shortly, it was nothing. Now it is growing something as we remember it. But still we know very little about it. What it will be when I remember it as I lie down to die, what it makes in me all my days till then—that is the real meeting. The other is only the beginning of it. You say you have poets in your world. Do they not teach you this?"

"Perhaps some of them do," said Ransom. "But even in a poem does a *hross* never long to hear one splendid line over again?"

Hyoi's reply unfortunately turned on one of those points in their language which Ransom had not mastered. There were two verbs which both, as far as he could see, meant to *long* or *yearn*; but the *hrossa* drew a sharp distinction, even an opposition, between them. Hyoi seemed to him merely to be saying that every one would long for it (*wondelone*) but no one in his senses could long for it (*hluntheline*).

"And indeed," he continued, "the poem is a good example. For the most splendid line becomes fully splendid only by means of all the lines after it; if you went back to it you would find it less splendid than you thought. You would kill it. I mean in a good poem."

"But in a bent poem, Hyoi?"

"A bent poem is not listened to, *Hmān.*"

"And how of love in a bent life?"

"How could the life of a *hnau* be bent?"

"Do you say, Hyoi, that there are no bent *hrossa?*"

Hyoi reflected. "I have heard," he said at last, "of something like what you mean. It is said that sometimes here and there a cub of certain age gets strange twists in him. I have heard of one that wanted to eat earth; there might, perhaps, be somewhere a *hross* likewise that wanted to have the years of love prolonged. I have not heard of it, but it might be. I have heard of something stranger. There is a poem about a *hross* who lived long ago, in another *handramit*, who saw things all made two—two suns in the sky, two heads on a neck; and last of all they say that he fell into such a frenzy that he desired two mates. I do not ask you to believe it, but that is the story: that he loved two *hressni.*"

Plato's Perfect City

CANTO I*

1

You stranger, long before your glance can light
Upon these words, time will have washed away
The moment when I first took pen to write,
With all my road before me—yet to-day,
Here, if at all, we meet; the unfashioned clay
Ready to both our hands; both hushed to see
That which is nowhere yet come forth and be.

2

This moment, if you join me, we begin
A partnership where both must toil to hold
The clue that I caught first. We lose or win
Together; if you read, you are enrolled.
And first, a marvel—Who could have foretold
That in the city which men called in scorn
The Perfect City, Dymer could be born?

3

There you'd have thought the gods were smothered down
Forever, and the keys were turned on fate.
No hour was left unchartered in that town,
And love was in a schedule and the State
Chose for eugenic reasons who should mate
With whom, and when. Each idle song and dance
Was fixed by law and nothing left to chance.

*From *Dymer*.

4

For some of the last Platonists had founded
That city of old. And masterly they made
An island of what ought to be, surrounded
By this gross world of easier light and shade.
All answering to the master's dream they laid
The strong foundations, torturing into stone
Each bubble that the Academy had blown.

5

This people were so pure, so law-abiding,
So logical, they made the heavens afraid:
They sent the very swallows into hiding
By their appalling chastity dismayed:
More soberly the lambs in spring-time played
Because of them: and ghosts dissolved in shame
Before their common-sense—till Dymer came.

6

At Dymer's birth no comets scared the nation,
The public crèche engulfed him with the rest,
And twenty separate Boards of Education
Closed round him. He passed through every test,
Was vaccinated, numbered, washed and dressed,
Proctored, inspected, whipt, examined weekly,
And for some nineteen years he bore it meekly.

7

For nineteen years they worked upon his soul,
Refining, chipping, moulding and adorning.
Then came the moment that undid the whole—
The ripple of rude life without a warning.
It came in lecture-time on April morning
—Alas for laws and locks, reproach and praise,
Who ever learned to censor the spring days?

8

A little breeze came stirring to his cheek.
He looked up to the window. A brown bird
Perched on the sill, bent down to whet his beak
With darting head—Poor Dymer watched and stirred
Uneasily. The lecturer's voice he heard
Still droning from the dais. The narrow room
Was drowsy, over-solemn, filled with gloom.

9

He yawned, and a voluptuous laziness
Tingled down all his spine and loosed his knees,
Slow-drawn, like an invisible caress.
He laughed—The lecturer stopped like one that sees
A Ghost, then frowned and murmured, "Silence, please."
That moment saw the soul of Dymer hang
In the balance—Louder then his laughter rang.

10

The whole room watched with unbelieving awe.
He rose and staggered rising. From his lips
Broke yet again the idiot-like guffaw.
He felt the spirit in his finger-tips,
Then swinging his right arm—a wide ellipse
Yet lazily—he struck the lecturer's head.
The old man tittered, lurched and dropt down dead.

11

Out of the silent room, out of the dark
Into the sun-stream Dymer passed, and there
The sudden breezes, the high-hanging lark,
The milk-white clouds sailing in polished air,
Suddenly flashed about him like a blare
Of trumpets. And no cry was raised behind him,
His class sat dazed. They dared not go to find him.

Nineteenth-Century Rationalism

ANOTHER TRAVELLER was already eating: he was a big man with red hair and a red stubble on all his three chins, buttoned up very tight. When they had both finished the traveller rose and cleared his throat and stood with his back to the fire. Then he cleared his throat again and said:

"A fine morning, young sir."

"Yes, sir," said John.

"You are going West, perhaps, young man?"

"I—I think so."

"It is possible that you don't know me."

"I am a stranger here."

"No offence," said the stranger. "My name is Mr. Enlightenment, and I believe it is pretty generally known. I shall be happy to give you my assistance and protection as far as our ways lie together."

John thanked him very much for this and when they went out from the inn there was a neat little trap waiting, with a fat little pony between the shafts: and its eyes were so bright and its harness was so well polished that it was difficult to say which was twinkling the keener in the morning sunshine. They both got into the trap and Mr. Enlightenment whipped up the fat little pony and they went bowling along the road as if nobody had a care in the world. Presently they began to talk.

"And where might you come from, my fine lad?" said Mr. Enlightenment.

"From Puritania, sir," said John.

"A good place to leave, eh?"

"I am so glad you think that," cried John. "I was afraid—"

"I hope I am a man of the world," said Mr. Enlightenment. "Any young fellow who is anxious to better himself may depend on finding sympathy and support in me. Puritania! Why, I suppose you have been brought up to be afraid of the Landlord."

"Well, I must admit I sometimes *do* feel rather nervous."

"You may make your mind easy, my boy. There is no such person."

"There is no Landlord?"

"There is absolutely no such thing—I might even say no such *entity*—in existence. There never has been and never will be."

"And is this absolutely certain?" cried John; for a great hope was rising in his heart.

"Absolutely certain. Look at me, young man. I ask you— do I look as if I was easily taken in?"

"Oh, no," said John hastily. "I was just wondering, though. I mean—how did they all come to think there was such a person?"

"The Landlord is an invention of those Stewards. All made up to keep the rest of us under their thumb: and of course the Stewards are hand in glove with the police. They are a shrewd lot, those Stewards. They know which side their bread is buttered on, all right. Clever fellows. Damn me, I can't help admiring them."

"But do you mean that the Stewards don't believe it themselves?"

"I dare say they do. It is just the sort of cock and bull story they would believe. They are simple old souls most of them—just like children. They have no knowledge of modern science and they would believe anything they were told."

John was silent for a few minutes. Then he began again:

"But how do you *know* there is no Landlord?"

"Christopher Columbus, Galileo, the earth is round, invention of printing, gunpowder!!" exclaimed Mr. Enlightenment in such a loud voice that the pony shied.

The Spirit of the Age

JOHN LAY IN HIS FETTERS all night in the cold and stench of the dungeon. And when morning came there was a little light at the grating, and, looking round, John saw that he had many fellow prisoners, of all sexes and ages. But instead of speaking to him, they all huddled away from the light and drew as far back into the pit, away from the grating, as they could. But John thought that if he could breathe a little fresh air he would be better, and he crawled up to the grating. But as soon as he looked out and saw the giant, it crushed the heart out of him: and even as he looked, the giant began to open his eyes and John, without knowing why he did it, shrank from the grating. Now I dreamed that the giant's eyes had this property, that whatever they looked on became transparent. Consequently, when John looked round into the dungeon, he retreated from his fellow prisoners in terror, for the place seemed to be thronged with demons. A woman was seated near him, but he did not know it was a woman, because, through the face, he saw the skull and through that the brains and the passages of the nose, and the larynx, and the saliva moving in the glands and the blood in the veins: and lower down the lungs panting like sponges, and the liver, and the intestines like a coil of snakes. And when he averted his eyes from her they fell on an old man, and this was worse for the old man had a cancer. And when John sat down and drooped his head, not to see the horrors, he saw only the working of his own inwards. Then I dreamed of all these creatures living in that hole under the giant's eye for many days and nights. And John looked round on it all and suddenly he fell on his face and thrust his hands into his eyes and cried out, "It is the black hole. There may be no Landlord, but it is true about the black hole. I am mad. I am dead. I am in hell for ever."

Science

THE PHYSICAL SCIENCES, good and innocent in themselves, had already, even in Ransom's own time, begun to be warped; had been subtly manœuvred in a certain direction. Despair of objective truth had been increasingly insinuated into the scientists; indifference to it, and a concentration upon mere power, had been the result. Babble about the *élan vital* and flirtations with panpsychism were bidding fair to restore the *Anima Mundi* of the magicians. Dreams of the far future destiny of man were dragging up from its shallow and unquiet grave the old dream of Man as God. The very experiences of the dissecting room and the pathological laboratory were breeding a conviction that the stifling of all deep-set repugnances was the first essential for progress. And now, all this had reached the stage at which its dark contrivers thought they could safely begin to bend it back so that it would meet that other and earlier kind of power. Indeed they were choosing the first moment at which this could have been done. You could not have done it with Nineteenth-Century scientists. Their firm objective materialism would have excluded it from their minds; and even if they could have been made to believe, their inherited morality would have kept them from touching dirt. MacPhee was a survivor from that tradition. It was different now. Perhaps few or none of the people at Belbury knew what was happening; but once it happened, they would be like straw in fire. What should they find incredible, since they believed no longer in a rational universe? What should they regard as too obscene, since they held that all morality was a mere subjective by-product of the physical and economic situations of men? The time was ripe. From the point of view which is accepted in Hell, the whole history of our Earth had led up to this moment. There was now at last a real chance for fallen Man to shake off that limitation of his powers which mercy had imposed upon him as a protection from the full results of his fall. If this succeeded, Hell would be at last incarnate. Bad men, while still in the body, still crawling on this little globe, would enter that state which, heretofore, they had entered only after death, would have the diuturnity and power of evil spirits. Nature, all over the globe of Tellus, would become their slave; and of that dominion no end, before the end of time itself, could be certainly foreseen.

Evolution

EVOLUTIONARY HYMN

Lead us, Evolution, lead us
  Up the future's endless stair:
Chop us, change us, prod us, weed us.
  For stagnation is despair:
Groping, guessing, yet progressing,
  Lead us nobody knows where.

Wrong or justice in the present,
  Joy or sorrow, what are they
While there's always jam to-morrow,
  While we tread the onward way?
Never knowing where we're going,
  We can never go astray.

To whatever variation
  Our posterity may turn
Hairy, squashy, or crustacean,
  Bulbous-eyed or square of stern,
Tusked or toothless, mild or ruthless,
  Towards that unknown god we yearn.

Ask not if it's god or devil,
  Brethren, lest your words imply
Static norms of good and evil
  (As in Plato) throned on high;
Such scholastic, inelastic,
  Abstract yardsticks we deny.

Far too long have sages vainly
  Glossed great Nature's simple text;

He who runs can read it plainly,
  "Goodness= what comes next."
By evolving, Life is solving
  All the questions we perplexed.

On then! Value means survival-
  Value. If our progeny
Spreads and spawns and licks each rival,
  That will prove its deity
(Far from pleasant, by our present
  Standards, though it well may be).

Freudianism

IN MY DREAM I saw them set off together, John walking by
the lạdy's stirrup: and I saw them go up the rocky valley
where John had gone on the night of his capture. They
found the pass unguarded and it gave back an echo to the
horse's hoofs and then in a moment they were out of the
mountain country and going down a grassy slope into the
land beyond. There were few trees and bare, and it was
cold: but presently John looked aside and saw a crocus in
the grass. For the first time for many days the old sweetness
pierced through John's heart: and the next moment he was
trying to call back the sound of the birds wheeling over the
Island and the green of the waves breaking on its sand—for
they had all flashed about him but so quickly that they were
gone before he knew. His eyes were wet.

He turned to Reason and spoke.

"You can tell me, lady. Is there such a place as the Island
in the West, or is it only a feeling of my own mind?"

"I cannot tell you," said she, "because you do not know."

"But you know."

"But I can tell you only what *you* know. I can bring things out of the dark part of your mind into the light part of it. But now you ask me what is not even in the dark part of your mind."

"Even if it were only a feeling in my own mind, would it be a bad feeling?"

"I have nothing to tell you of good and bad."

"I mean this," said John. "And this you can tell me. Is it true that it must always end in brown girls, or rather, that it really *begins* from brown girls? They say it is all a pretence, all a disguise for lust."

"And what do you think of that saying?"

"It is very like that," said John. "Both are sweet. Both are full of longing. The one turns into the other. They *are* very alike."

"Indeed they are," said the lady. "But do you not remember my third riddle?"

"About the copy and the original? I could not understand it."

"Well, now you shall. The people in the country we have just left have seen that your love for the Island is very like your love for the brown girls. Therefore they say that one is a copy of the other. They would also say that you have followed me because I am like your mother, and that your trust in me is a copy of your love for your mother. And then they would say again that your love for your mother is a copy of your love for the brown girls; and so they would come full circle."

"And what should I answer them?"

"You would say, perhaps one is a copy of the other. But which is the copy of which?"

"I never thought of that."

"You are not yet of an age to have thought much," said Reason. "But you must see that if two things are alike, then it is a further question whether the first is copied from the second, or the second from the first, or both from a third."

"What would the third be?"

"Some have thought that all these loves were copies of our love for the Landlord."

"But surely they have considered that and rejected it. Their sciences have disproved it."

"They could not have, for their sciences are not concerned at all with the general relations of this country to anything that may lie East of it or West of it. They indeed will tell you that their researches have proved that if two things are similar, the fair one is always the copy of the foul one. But their only reason to say so is that they have already decided that the fairest things of all—that is the Landlord, and, if you like, the mountains and the Island—are a mere copy of *this* country. They pretend that their researches lead to the doctrine: but in fact they assume that doctrine first and interpret their researches by it."

"But they have reasons for assuming it."

"They have none, for they have ceased to listen to the only people who can tell them anything about it."

"Who are they?"

"They are younger sisters of mine, and their names are Philosophy and Theology."

Progressive Education

IT WAS A DULL AUTUMN DAY and Jill Pole was crying behind the gym.

She was crying because they had been bullying her. This is not going to be a school story, so I shall say as little as possible about Jill's school, which is not a pleasant subject. It was "Co-educational," a school for both boys and girls, what used to be called a "mixed" school; some said it was not nearly so mixed as the minds of the people who ran it.

These people had the idea that boys and girls should be allowed to do what they liked. And unfortunately what ten or fifteen of the biggest boys and girls liked best was bullying the others. All sorts of things, horrid things, went on which at an ordinary school would have been found out and stopped in half a term; but at this school they weren't. Or even if they were, the people who did them were not expelled or punished. The Head said they were interesting psychological cases and sent for them and talked to them for hours. And if you knew the right sort of things to say to the Head, the main result was that you became rather a favourite than otherwise.

That was why Jill Pole was crying on that dull autumn day on the damp little path which runs between the back of the gym and the shrubbery. And she hadn't nearly finished her cry when a boy came round the corner of the gym whistling, with his hands in his pockets. He nearly ran into her.

"Can't you look where you're going?" said Jill Pole.

"All *right*," said the boy, "you needn't start—" and then he noticed her face. "I say, Pole," he said, "what's up?"

Jill only made faces; the sort you make when you're trying to say something but find that if you speak you'll start crying again.

"It's *Them*, I suppose—as usual," said the boy grimly, digging his hands further into his pockets.

Jill nodded. There was no need for her to say anything, even if she could have said it. They both knew.

"Now, look here," said the boy, "there's no good us all—"

He meant well but he *did* talk rather like someone beginning a lecture. Jill suddenly flew into a temper (which is quite a likely thing to happen if you have been interrupted in a cry).

"Oh, go away and mind your own business," she said. "Nobody asked you to come barging in, did they? And you're a nice person to start telling us what we all ought to do, aren't you? I suppose you mean we ought to spend all our time sucking up to Them, and currying favour, and dancing attendance on Them like you do."

"Oh, Lor!" said the boy, sitting down on the grassy bank at the edge of the shrubbery and very quickly getting up again because the grass was soaking wet. His name unfortunately was Eustace Scrubb, but he wasn't a bad sort.

"Pole!" he said. "Is that fair? Have I been doing anything of the sort this term? Didn't I stand up to Carter about the rabbit? And didn't I keep the secret about Spivvins—under torture too? And didn't I—"

"I d-don't know and I don't care," sobbed Jill.

Scrubb saw that she wasn't quite herself yet and very sensibly offered her a peppermint. He had one too. Presently Jill began to see things in a clearer light.

"I'm sorry, Scrubb," she said presently. "I wasn't fair. You have done all that—this term."

"Then wash out last term if you can," said Eustace. "I was a different chap then. I was—gosh! what a little tick I was."

"Well, honestly, you were," said Jill.

"You think there has been a change, then?" said Eustace.

"It's not only me," said Jill. "Everyone's been saying so. *They've* noticed it. Eleanor Blakiston heard Adela Pennyfather talking about it in our changing room yesterday. She said, Someone's got hold of that Scrubb kid. He's quite unmanageable this term. We shall have to attend to *him* next.' "

Eustace gave a shudder. Everyone at Experiment House knew what it was like being "attended to" by *Them*.

Reason

REASON

Set on the soul's acropolis the reason stands
A virgin, arm'd, commercing with celestial light,
And he who sins against her has defiled his own
Virginity: no cleansing makes his garment white;
So clear is reason. But how dark imagining,
Warm, dark, obscure and infinite, daughter of Night:
Dark is her brow, the beauty of her eyes with sleep
Is loaded, and her pains are long, and her delight.
Tempt not Athene. Wound not in her fertile pains
Demeter, nor rebel against her mother-right.
Oh who will reconcile in me both maid and mother,
Who make in me a concord of the depth and height?
Who make imagination's dim exploring touch
Ever report the same as intellectual sight?
Then could I truly say, and not deceive,
Then wholly say, that I BELIEVE.

Reason the Giant Slayer

WHEN THEY CAME OUT into the air John blinked a little but
not much, for they were still only in a half-light under the
shadow of the giant, who was very angry, with smoke coming from his mouth, so that he looked more like a volcano
than an ordinary mountain. And now John gave himself up
for lost, but just as the jailor had dragged him up to the
giant's feet, and had cleared his throat, and begun "The

case against this prisoner—" there was a commotion and a sound of horse's hoofs. The jailor looked round, and even the giant took his terrible eyes off John and looked round: and last of all, John himself looked round too. They saw some of the guard coming towards them leading a great black stallion, and in it was seated a figure wound in a cloak of blue which was hooded over the head and came down concealing the face.

"Another prisoner, Lord," said the leader of the guards.

Then very slowly the giant raised his great, heavy finger and pointed to the mouth of the dungeon.

"Not yet," said the hooded figure. Then suddenly it stretched out its hands with the fetters on them and made a quick movement of the wrists. There was a tinkling sound as the fragments of the broken chain fell on the rock at the horse's feet: and the guardsmen let go the bridle and fell back, watching. Then the rider threw back the cloak and a flash of steel smote light into John's eyes and on the giant's face. John saw that it was a woman in the flower of her age: she was so tall that she seemed to him a Titaness, a sun-bright virgin clad in complete steel, with a sword naked in her hand. The giant bent forward in his chair and looked at her.

"Who are you?" he said.

"My name is Reason," said the virgin.

"Make out her passport quickly," said the giant in a low voice. "And let her go through our dominions and be off with all the speed she wishes."

"Not yet," said Reason. "I will ask you three riddles before I go, for a wager."

"What is the pledge?" said the giant.

"Your head," said Reason.

There was silence for a time among the mountains.

"Well," said the giant at last, "what must be, must be. Ask on."

"This is my first riddle," said Reason. "What is the colour

of things in dark places, of fish in the depth of the sea, or of the entrails in the body of man?"

"I cannot say," said the giant.

"Well," said Reason. "Now hear my second riddle. There was a certain man who was going to his own house and his enemy went with him. And his house was beyond a river too swift to swim and too deep to wade. And he could go no faster than his enemy. While he was on his journey his wife sent to him and said, You know that there is only one bridge across the river: tell me, shall I destroy it that the enemy may not cross; or shall I leave it standing that you may cross? What should this man do?"

"It is too hard for me," said the giant.

"Well," said Reason. "Try now to answer my third riddle. By what rule do you tell a copy from an original?"

The giant muttered and mumbled and could not answer, and Reason set spurs in her stallion and it leaped up on to the giant's mossy knees and galloped up his foreleg, till she plunged her sword into his heart. Then there was a noise and a crumbling like a landslide and the huge carcass settled down; and the Spirit of the Age became what he had seemed to be at first, a sprawling hummock of rock.

The Imagined Terrors of Malacandra

THOUGH HE KNEW that it would be prudent to return to his bed as quickly as possible, he found himself standing still in the now familiar glory of the light and viewing it with a new and poignant emotion. Out of this heaven, these happy climes, they were presently to descend—into *what?* *Sorns*, human sacrifice, loathsome sexless monsters. What

was a *sorn?* His own role in the affair was now clear
enough. Somebody or something had sent for him. It could
hardly be for him personally. The somebody wanted a victim—any victim—from Earth. He had been picked because
Devine had done the picking; he realized for the first time—
in all circumstances a late and startling discovery—that Devine had hated him all these years as heartily as he hated
Devine. But what was a *sorn?* "When he saw them he
would eat out of Devine's hands." His mind, like so many
minds of his generation, was richly furnished with bogies.
He had read his H. G. Wells and others. His universe was
peopled with horrors such as ancient and mediæval mythology could hardly rival. No insect-like, vermiculate or
crustacean Abominable, no twitching feelers, rasping
wings, slimy coils, curling tentacles, no monstrous union of
superhuman intelligence and insatiable cruelty seemed to
him anything but likely on an alien world. The *sorns* would
be . . . would be . . . he dared not think what the *sorns*
would be. And he was to be given to them. Somehow this
seemed more horrible than being caught by them. Given,
handed over, offered. He saw in imagination various in-
compatible monstrosities—bulbous eyes, grinning jaws,
horns, stings, mandibles. Loathing of insects, loathing of
snakes, loathing of things that squashed and squelched, all
played their horrible symphonies over his nerves. But the
reality would be worse: it would be an extra-terrestrial Oth-
erness—something one had never thought of, never could
have thought of. In that moment Ransom made a decision.
He could face death, but not the *sorns.* He must escape
when they got to Malacandra, if there were any possibility.
Starvation, or even to be chased by *sorns,* would be better
than being handed over. If escape were impossible, then it
must be suicide. Ransom was a pious man. He hoped he
would be forgiven. It was no more in his power, he
thought, to decide otherwise than to grow a new limb.
Without hesitation he stole back into the galley and secured

the sharpest knife: henceforward he determined never to be parted from it.

First Glimpse of Malacandra

NATURALLY ENOUGH all he saw was the ground—a circle of pale pink, almost white: whether very close and short vegetation or very wrinkled and granulated rock or soil he could not say. Instantly the dark shape of Devine filled the aperture, and Ransom had time to notice that he had a revolver in his hand—"For me or for *sorns* or for both?" he wondered.

"You next," said Weston curtly.

Ransom took a deep breath and his hand went to the knife beneath his belt. Then he got his head and shoulders through the manhole, his two hands on the soil of Malacandra. The pink stuff was soft and faintly resilient, like india-rubber; clearly vegetation. Instantly Ransom looked up. He saw a pale blue sky—a fine winter-morning sky it would have been on Earth—a great billowy cumular mass of rose-colour lower down which he took for a cloud, and then—

"Get out," said Weston from behind him.

He scrambled through and rose to his feet. The air was cold but not bitterly so, and it seemed a little rough at the back of his throat. He gazed about him, and the very intensity of his desire to take in the new world at a glance defeated itself. He saw nothing but colours—colours that refused to form themselves into things. Moreover, he knew nothing yet well enough to see it: you cannot see things till you know roughly what they are. His first impression was of a bright, pale world—a water-colour world out of child's paint-box; a moment later he recognized the flat belt of light blue as a sheet of water, or of something like water, which

came nearly to his feet. They were on the shore of a lake or
river.

Closer View of Malacandra

ON ONE SIDE the water extended a long way—about a
quarter of a mile, he thought, but perspective was still difficult in the strange world. On the other side it was much
narrower, not wider than fifteen feet perhaps, and seemed
to be flowing over a shallow—broken and swirling water
that made a softer and more hissing sound than water on
Earth; and where it washed the hither bank—the pinkish-
white vegetation went down to the very brink—there was
a bubbling and sparkling which suggested effervescence.
He tried hard, in such stolen glances as the work allowed
him, to make out something of the farther shore. A mass of
something purple, so huge that he took it for a heather-cov-
ered mountain, was his first impression: on the other side,
beyond the larger water, there was something of the same
kind. But there, he could see over the top of it. Beyond were
strange upright shapes of whitish green: too jagged and
irregular for buildings, too thin and steep for mountains.
Beyond and above these again was the rose-coloured cloud-
like mass. It might really be a cloud, but it was very solid-
looking and did not seem to have moved since he first set
eyes on it from the manhole. It looked like the top of a gigantic red cauliflower—or like a huge bowl of red soap-
suds—and it was exquisitely beautiful in tint and shape.

Baffled by this, he turned his attention to the nearer shore
beyond the shallows. The purple mass looked for a moment
like a plump of organ-pipes, then like a stack of rolls of
cloth set up on end, then like a forest of gigantic umbrellas
blown inside out. It was in faint motion. Suddenly his eyes

mastered the object. The purple stuff was vegetation: more precisely it was vegetables, vegetables about twice the height of English elms, but apparently soft and flimsy. The stalks—one could hardly call them trunks—rose smooth and round, and surprisingly thin, for about forty feet: above that, the huge plants opened into a sheaf-like development, not of branches but of leaves, leaves large as lifeboats but nearly transparent. The whole thing corresponded roughly to his idea of a submarine forest: the plants, at once so large and so frail, seemed to need water to support them, and he wondered that they could hang in the air. Lower down, between the stems, he saw the vivid purple twilight, mottled with paler sunshine, which made up the internal scenery of the wood.

First Glimpse of Perelandra

HIS FIRST IMPRESSION was of nothing more definite than of something slanted—as though he were looking at a photograph which had been taken when the camera was not held level. And even this lasted only for an instant. The slant was replaced by a different slant; then two slants rushed together and made a peak, and the peak flattened suddenly into a horizontal line, and the horizontal line tilted and became the edge of a vast gleaming slope which rushed furiously towards him. At the same moment he felt that he was being lifted. Up and up he soared till it seemed as if he must reach the burning dome of gold that hung above him instead of a sky. Then he was at a summit; but almost before his glance had taken in a huge valley that yawned beneath him—shining green like glass and marbled with streaks of scummy white—he was rushing down into that valley at perhaps thirty miles an hour. And now he realised that there was a delicious coolness over every part of him except his head, that his feet rested on nothing, and that he had for some time been performing unconsciously the actions of a swimmer. He was riding the foamless swell of an ocean, fresh and cool after the fierce temperatures of Heaven, but warm by earthly standards—as warm as a shallow bay with sandy bottom in a sub-tropical climate. As he rushed smoothly up the great convex hillside of the next wave he got a mouthful of the water. It was hardly at all flavoured with salt; it was drinkable—like fresh water and only, by an infinitesimal degree, less insipid. Though he had not been aware of thirst till now, his drink gave him a quite astonishing pleasure. It was almost like meeting Pleasure itself for the first time. He buried his flushed face in the green translucence, and when he withdrew it, found himself once more on the top of a wave.

There was no land in sight. The sky was pure, flat gold like the background of a medieval picture. It looked very distant—as far off as a cirrhus cloud looks from earth. The ocean was gold too, in the offing, flecked with innumerable shadows. The nearer waves, though golden where their summits caught the light, were green on their slopes: first emerald, and lower down a lustrous bottle green, deepening to blue where they passed beneath the shadow of other waves.

All this he saw in a flash; then he was speeding down once more into the trough. He had somehow turned on his back. He saw the golden roof of that world quivering with a rapid variation of paler lights as a ceiling quivers at the reflected sunlight from the bath-water when you step into your bath on a summer morning. He guessed that this was the reflection of the waves wherein he swam. It is a phenomenon observable three days out of five in the planet of love. The queen of those seas views herself continually in a celestial mirror.

Up again to the crest, and still no sight of land. Something that looked like clouds—or could it be ships?—far away on his left. Then down, down, down—he thought he would never reach the end of it . . . this time he noticed how dim the light was. Such tepid revelry in water—such glorious bathing, as one would have called it on earth, suggested as its natural accompaniment a blazing sun. But here there was no such thing. The water gleamed, the sky burned with gold, but all was rich and dim, and his eyes fed upon it undazzled and unaching. The very names of green and gold, which he used perforce in describing the scene, are too harsh for the tenderness, the muted iridescence, of that warm, maternal, delicately glorious world. It was mild to look upon as evening, warm like summer noon, gentle and winning like early dawn. It was altogether pleasurable. He sighed.

Cosmic Imperialism

"Speak to Ransom, and he shall turn it into our speech," said Oyarsa.

Weston accepted the arrangement at once. He believed that the hour of his death was come and he was determined to utter the thing—almost the only thing outside his own science—which he had to say. He cleared his throat, almost he struck a gesture, and began:

"To you I may seem a vulgar robber, but I bear on my shoulders the destiny of the human race. Your tribal life with its stone-age weapons and bee-hive huts, its primitive coracles and elementary social structure, has nothing to compare with our civilization—with our science, medicine and law, our armies, our architecture, our commerce, and our transport system which is rapidly annihilating space and time. Our right to supersede you is the right of the higher over the lower. Life——"

"Half a moment," said Ransom in English. "That's about as much as I can manage at one go." Then, turning to Oyarsa, he began translating as well as he could. The process was difficult and the result—which he felt to be rather unsatisfactory—was something like this:

"Among us, Oyarsa, there is a kind of *hnau* who will take other *hnau's* food and—and things, when they are not looking. He says he is not an ordinary one of that kind. He says what he does now will make very different things happen to those of our people who are not yet born. He says that, among you, *hnau* of one kindred all live together and the *hrossa* have spears like those we used a very long time ago and your huts are small and round and your boats small and light and like our old ones, and you have only one ruler. He says it is different with us. He says we know much. There is a thing happens in our world when the body of a living creature feels pains and becomes weak, and he says we sometimes know how to stop it. He says we have many bent people and we kill them or shut them in huts and that we have people for settling quarrels between the bent *hnau* about their huts and mates and things. He says we have many ways for the *hnau* of one land to kill those of another and some are trained to do it. He says we build very big and strong huts of stones and other things— like the *pfifltriggi*. And he says we exchange many things among ourselves and can carry heavy weights very quickly a long way. Because of all this, he says it would not be the act of a bent *hnau* if our people killed all your people."

As soon as Ransom finished, Weston continued.

"Life is greater than any system of morality; her claims are absolute. It is not by tribal taboos and copy-book maxims that she has pursued her relentless march from the amœba to man and from man to civilization."

"He says," began Ransom, "that living creatures are

stronger than the question whether an act is bent or good—
no, that cannot be right—he says it is better to be alive and
bent than to be dead—no—he says, he says—I cannot say
what he says, Oyarsa, in your language. But he goes on to
say that the only good thing is that there should be very
many creatures alive. He says there were many other animals before the first men and the later ones were better than
the earlier ones; but he says the animals were not born because of what is said to the young about bent and good
action by their elders. And he says these animals did not
feel any pity."

Encounter with a Goddess

A FLAME COLOURED robe, in which her hands were hidden,
covered this person from the feet to where it rose behind
her neck in a kind of high ruff-like collar, but in front it was
so low or open that it exposed her large breasts. Her skin
was darkish and Southern and glowing, almost the colour
of honey. Some such dress Jane had seen worn by a Minoan
priestess on a vase from old Cnossus. The head, poised motionless on the muscular pillar of her neck, stared straight at
Jane. It was a red-cheeked, wet-lipped face, with black
eyes—almost the eyes of a cow—and an enigmatic expression. It was not by ordinary standards at all like the face of
Mother Dimble; but Jane recognised it at once. It was, to
speak like the musicians, the full statement of that theme
which had elusively haunted Mother Dimble's face for the
last few hours. It was Mother Dimble's face with something
left out, and the omission shocked Jane. "It is brutal," she
thought, for its energy crushed her; but then she half
changed her mind and thought, "It is I who am weak, trumpery." "It is mocking me," she thought, but then once more

changed her mind and thought, "It is ignoring me. It doesn't see me"; for though there was an almost ogre-ish glee in the face, Jane did not seem to be invited to share the joke. She tried to look aside from the face—succeeded—and saw for the first time that there were other creatures present—four or five of them—no, more—a whole crowd of ridiculous little men: fat dwarfs in red caps with tassels on them, chubby, gnome-like little men, quite insufferably familiar, frivolous, and irrepressible. For there was no doubt that they, at any rate, were mocking her. They were pointing at her, nodding, mimicking, standing on their heads, turning somersaults. Jane was not yet frightened, partly because the extreme warmth of the air at this open window made her feel drowsy. It was really quite ridiculous for the time of year. Her main feeling was one of indignation. A suspicion which had crossed her mind once or twice before now returned to her with irresistible force—the suspicion that the real universe might be simply silly. It was closely mixed up with the memories of that grown-up laughter— loud, careless, masculine laughter on the lips of bachelor uncles—which had often infuriated her in childhood, and from which the intense seriousness of her school debating society had offered such a grateful escape.

But a moment later she was very frightened indeed. The giantess rose. They were all coming at her. With a great glow and a noise like fire the flame-robed woman and the malapert dwarfs had all come into the house. They were in the room with her. The strange woman had a torch in her hand. It burned with terrible, blinding brightness, crackling, and sent up a cloud of dense black smoke, and filled the bedroom with a sticky, resinous smell. "If they're not careful," thought Jane, "they'll set the house on fire."

Hell

WE MUST PICTURE Hell as a state where everyone is perpetually concerned about his own dignity and advancement, where everyone has a grievance, and where everyone lives the deadly serious passions of envy, self-importance, and resentment. This, to begin with. For the rest, my own choice of symbols depended, I suppose, on temperament and on the age.

I like bats much better than bureaucrats. I live in the Managerial Age, in a world of "Admin." The greatest evil is not now done in those sordid "dens of crime" that Dickens loved to paint. It is not done even in concentration camps and labour camps. In those we see its final result. But it is conceived and ordered (moved, seconded, carried, and minuted) in clean, carpeted, warmed, and well-lighted offices, by quiet men with white collars and cut fingernails and smooth-shaven cheeks who do not need to raise their voice. Hence, naturally enough, my symbol for Hell is something like the bureaucracy of a police state or the offices of a thoroughly nasty business concern.

Milton has told us that "devil with devil damned Firm concord holds." But how? Certainly not by friendship. A being which can still love is not yet a devil. Here again my symbol seemed to me useful. It enabled me, by earthly parallels, to picture an official society held together entirely by fear and greed. On the surface, manners are normally suave. Rudeness to one's superiors would obviously be suicidal; rudeness to one's equals might put them on their guard before you were ready to spring your mine. For of course "Dog eat dog" is the principle of the whole organisation. Everyone wishes everyone else's discrediting, demotion, and ruin; everyone is an expert in the confidential report, the pretended alliance, the stab in the back. Over all this their good manners, their expressions of grave respect, their "tributes" to one another's invaluable services form a thin crust. Every now and then it gets punctured, and the scalding lava of their hatred spurts out.

This symbol also enabled me to get rid of the absurd fancy that devils are engaged in the disinterested pursuit of something called Evil (the capital is essential). Mine have no use for any such turnip ghost. Bad angels, like bad men, are entirely practical. They have two motives. The first is fear of punishment: for as totalitarian countries have their camps for torture, so my Hell contains deeper Hells, its "houses of correction." Their second motive is a kind of hunger. I feign that devils can, in a spiritual sense, eat one another; and us. Even in human life we have seen the passion to dominate, almost to digest, one's fellow; to make his whole intellectual and emotional life merely an extension of one's own—to hate one's hatreds and resent one's grievances and indulge one's egoism through him as well as through oneself. His own little store of passion must of course be suppressed to make room for ours. If he resists this suppression he is being very selfish.

On Earth this desire is often called "love." In Hell I feign that they recognise it as hunger. But there the hunger is more ravenous, and a fuller satisfaction is possible. There, I suggest, the stronger spirit—there are perhaps no bodies to impede the operation—can really and irrevocably suck the weaker into itself and permanently gorge its own being on the weaker's outraged individuality. It is (I feign) for this that devils desire human souls and the souls of one another. It is for this that Satan desires all his own followers and all of the sons of Eve and all the host of Heaven. His dream is of the day when all shall be inside him and all that says "I" can say it only through him. This, I surmise, is the bloated-spider parody, the only imitation he can understand, of that unfathomed bounty whereby God turns tools into servants and servants into sons, so that they may be at last reunited to Him in the perfect freedom of a love offered from the height of the utter individualities which he has liberated them to be.

The Wisdom of Screwtape on Mutual Annoyance

MY DEAR WORMWOOD, I am very pleased by what you tell me about this man's relations with his mother. But you must press your advantage. The Enemy will be working from the centre outwards, gradually bringing more and more of the patient's conduct under the new standard, and may reach his behaviour to the old lady at any moment. You want to get in first. Keep in close touch with our colleague Glubose who is in charge of the mother, and build up between you in that house a good settled habit of mutual annoyance: daily pinpricks. The following methods are useful.

1. Keep his mind on the inner life. He thinks his conversion is something *inside* him and his attention is therefore chiefly turned at present to the states of his own mind—or rather to that very expurgated version of them which is all you should allow him to see. Encourage this. Keep his mind off the most elementary duties by directing it to the most advanced and spiritual ones. Aggravate that most useful human characteristic, the horror and neglect of the obvious. You must bring him to a condition in which he can practise self-examination for an hour without discovering any of those facts about himself which are perfectly clear to anyone who has ever lived in the same house with him or worked in the same office.

2. It is, no doubt, impossible to prevent his praying for his mother, but we have means of rendering the prayers innocuous. Make sure that they are always very "spiritual," that he is always concerned with the state of her soul and never with her rheumatism. Two advantages will follow. In the first place, his attention will be kept on what he regards as her sins, by which, with a little guidance from you, he can be induced to mean any of her actions which are inconvenient or irritating to himself. Thus you can keep rubbing the wounds of the day a little sorer even while he is on his knees; the operation is not at all difficult and you will find it very entertaining. In the second place, since his ideas about her soul will be very crude and often erroneous, he will, in some degree, be praying for an imaginary person, and it will be your task to make that imaginary person daily less and less like the real mother—the sharp-tongued old lady at the breakfast table. In time, you may get the cleavage so wide that no thought or feeling from his prayers for the imagined mother will ever flow over into his treatment of the real one. I have had patients of my own so well in hand that they could be turned at a moment's notice from impassioned prayer for a wife's or son's "soul" to beating or insulting the real wife or son without a qualm.

3. When two humans have lived together for many years, it usually happens that each has tones of voice and expressions of face which are almost unendurably irritating to the other. Work on that. Bring fully into the consciousness of your patient that particular lift of his mother's eyebrows which he learned to dislike in the nursery, and let him think how much he dislikes it. Let him assume that she knows how annoying it is and does it to annoy—if you know your job he will not notice the immense improbability of the assumption. And, of course, never let him suspect that he has tones and looks which similarly annoy her. As he cannot see or hear himself, this is easily managed.

4. In civilised life domestic hatred usually expresses itself

by saying things which would appear quite harmless on paper (the *words* are not offensive) but in such a voice, or at such a moment, that they are not far short of a blow in the face. To keep this game up you and Glubose must see to it that each of these two fools has a sort of double standard. Your patient must demand that all his own utterances are to be taken at their face value and judged simply on the actual words, while at the same time judging all his mother's utterances with the fullest and most oversensitive interpretation of the tone and the context and the suspected intention. She must be encouraged to do the same to him. Hence from every quarrel they can both go away convinced, or very nearly convinced, that they are quite innocent. You know the kind of thing: "I simply ask her what time dinner will be and she flies into a temper." Once this habit is well established you have the delightful situation of a human saying things with the express purpose of offending and yet having a grievance when offence is taken.

The Wisdom of Screwtape on Conscientious Objectors

IF YOUR PATIENT can be induced to become a conscientious objector he will automatically find himself one of a small, vocal, organised, and unpopular society, and the effects of this, on one so new to Christianity, will almost certainly be good. But only *almost* certainly. Has he had serious doubts about the lawfulness of serving in a just war before this present war began? Is he a man of great physical courage—so great that he will have no half-conscious misgivings about the real motives of his pacifism? Can he, when nearest to honesty (no human is ever *very* near), feel fully convinced that he is actuated wholly by the desire to obey the Enemy? If he is that sort of man, his pacifism will probably not do us much good, and the Enemy will probably protect him from the usual consequences of belonging to a sect. Your best plan, in that case, would be to attempt a sudden, confused, emotional crisis from which he might emerge as an uneasy convert to patriotism. Such things can often be managed. But if he is the man I take him to be, try Pacifism.

The Wisdom of Screwtape on Church Factions

THE TWO CHURCHES nearest to him, I have looked up in the office. Both have certain claims. At the first of these the vicar is a man who has been so long engaged in watering down the faith to make it easier for a supposedly incredulous and hardheaded congregation that it is now he who shocks his parishioners with his unbelief, not vice versa. He has undermined many a soul's Christianity. His conduct of the services is also admirable. In order to spare the laity all "difficulties" he has deserted both the lectionary and the appointed psalms and now, without noticing it, revolves endlessly round the little treadmill of his fifteen favourite psalms and twenty favourite lessons. We are thus safe from the danger that any truth not already familiar to him and to his flock should ever reach them through Scripture. But perhaps your patient is not quite silly enough for this church— or not yet?

At the other church we have Fr. Spike. The humans are often puzzled to understand the range of his opinions— why he is one day almost a Communist and the next not far from some kind of theocratic Fascism—one day a scholastic,

and the next prepared to deny human reason altogether—
one day immersed in politics, and, the day after, declaring
that all states of this world are *equally* "under judgment."
We, of course, see the connecting link, which is Hatred.
The man cannot bring himself to preach anything which is
not calculated to shock, grieve, puzzle, or humiliate his parents and their friends. A sermon which such people. could
accept would be to him as insipid as a poem which they
could scan. There is also a promising streak of dishonesty
in him; we are teaching him to say "The teaching of the
Church is" when he really means "I'm almost sure I read
recently in Maritain or someone of that sort." But I must
warn you that he has one fatal defect: he really believes.
And this may yet mar all.

But there is one good point which both these churches
have in common—they are both party churches. I think I
warned you before that if your patient can't be kept out of
the Church, he ought at least to be violently attached to
some party within it. I don't mean on really doctrinal is-
sues; about those, the more lukewarm he is, the better. And
it isn't the doctrines on which we chiefly depend for producing malice. The real fun is working up hatred between
those who *say* "mass" and those who *say* "holy commun-
ion" when neither party could possibly state the difference
between, say, Hooker's doctrine and Thomas Aquinas', in
any form which would hold water for five minutes. And all
the purely indifferent things—candles and clothes and what
not—are an admirable ground for our activities. We have
quite removed from men's minds what that pestilent fellow
Paul used to teach about food and other unessentials—
namely, that the human without scruples should always
give in to the human with scruples. You would think they
could not fail to see the application. You would expect to
find the "low" churchman genuflecting and crossing himself lest the weak conscience of his "high" brother should

be moved to irreverence, and the "high" one refraining from these exercises lest he should betray his "low" brother into idolatry. And so it would have been but for our ceaseless labour. Without that, the variety of usage within the Church of England might have become a positive hotbed of charity and humility.

Your affectionate uncle
SCREWTAPE

The Wisdom of Screwtape on Marriage

HIS REAL MOTIVE for fixing on sex as the method of reproduction among humans is only too apparent from the use He has made of it. Sex might have been, from our point of view, quite innocent. It might have been merely one more mode in which a stronger self preyed upon a weaker—as it is, indeed, among the spiders where the bride concludes her nuptials by eating her groom. But in the humans the Enemy has gratuitously associated affection between the parties with sexual desire. He has also made the offspring dependent on the parents and given the parents an impulse to support it—thus producing the Family, which is like the organism, only worse; for the members are more distinct, yet also united in a more conscious and responsible way. The whole thing, in fact, turns out to be simply one more device for dragging in Love.

Now comes the joke. The Enemy described a married couple as "one flesh." He did not say "a happily married couple" or "a couple who married because they were in love," but you can make the humans ignore that. You can also make them forget that the man they call Paul did not confine it to *married* couples. Mere copulation, for him, makes "one flesh." You can thus get the humans to accept as rhetorical eulogies of "being in love" what were in fact plain descriptions of the real significance of sexual intercourse. The truth is that wherever a man lies with a woman, there, whether they like it or not, a transcendental relation is set up between them which must be eternally enjoyed or eternally endured. From the true statement that this transcendental relation was intended to produce—and, if obediently entered into, too often *will* produce—affection and the family, humans can be made to infer the false belief that the blend of affection, fear, and desire which they call "being in love" is the only thing that makes marriage either happy or holy. The error is easy to produce because "being in love" does very often, in western Europe, precede marriages which are made in obedience to the Enemy's designs, that is, with the intention of fidelity, fertility, and goodwill; just as religious emotion very often, but not always, attends conversion. In other words, the humans are to be encouraged to regard as the basis for marriage a highly coloured and distorted version of something the Enemy really promises as its result. Two advantages follow. In the first place, humans who have not the gift of continence can be deterred from seeking marriage as a solution because they do not find themselves "in love," and, thanks to us, the idea of marrying with any other motive seems to them low and cynical. Yes, they think that. They regard the intention of loyalty to a partnership for mutual help, for the preservation of chastity, and for the transmission of life, as something lower than a storm of emotion. (Don't neglect to make your man think the marriage service very offensive.) In the second place any sexual infatuation whatever, so long as it intends marriage, will be regarded as "love," and "love" will be held to excuse a man from all the guilt, and to protect him from all the consequences, of marrying a heathen, a fool, or a wanton. . . .

Your affectionate uncle

SCREWTAPE

The Wisdom of Screwtape on the Terrestrial Venus and the Infernal Venus

YOU WILL FIND, if you look carefully into any human's heart, that he is haunted by at least two imaginary women—a terrestrial and an infernal Venus, and that his desire differs qualitatively according to its object. There is one type for which his desire is such as to be naturally amenable to the Enemy—readily mixed with charity, readily obedient to marriage, coloured all through with that golden light of reverence and naturalness which we detest; there is another type which he desires brutally, and desires to desire brutally, a type best used to draw him away from marriage altogether but which, even within marriage, he would tend to treat as a slave, an idol, or an accomplice. His love for the first might involve what the Enemy calls evil, but only accidentally; the man would wish that she was not someone else's wife and be sorry that he could not love her lawfully. But in the second type, the felt evil is what he wants; it is that "tang" in the flavour which he is after. In the face, it is the visible animality, or sulkiness or craft or cruelty, which he likes, and in the body, something quite different from what he ordinarily calls Beauty, something he may even, in a sane hour, describe as ugliness, but which, by our art, can be made to play on the raw nerve of his private obsession.

The real use of the infernal Venus is, no doubt, as prostitute or mistress. But if your man is a Christian, and if he has been well trained in nonsense about irresistible and all-excusing "Love," he can often be induced to marry her. And that is very well worth bringing about. You will have failed as regards fornication and solitary vice; but there are other, and more indirect, methods of using a man's sexuality to his undoing. And, by the way, they are not only efficient, but delightful; the unhappiness produced is of a very lasting and exquisite kind.

Your affectionate uncle

SCREWTAPE

The Wisdom of Screwtape on the Christian Home

THEN, OF COURSE, he gets to know this woman's family and whole circle. Could you not see that the very house she lives in is one that he ought never to have entered? The whole place reeks of that deadly odour. The very gardener, though he has been there only five years, is beginning to acquire it. Even guests, after a weekend visit, carry some of the smell away with them. The dog and the cat are tainted with it. And a house full of the impenetrable mystery. We are certain (it is a matter of first principles) that each member of the family must in some way be making capital out of the others—but we can't find out how. They guard as jealously as the Enemy Himself the secret of what really lies behind this pretence of disinterested love. The whole house and garden are one vast obscenity. It bears a sickening resemblance to the description one human writer made of

Heaven: "the regions where there is only life and therefore all that is not music is silence."

The Wisdom of Screwtape on the "Historical Jesus"

YOU WILL FIND that a good many Christian political writers think that Christianity began going wrong, and departing from the doctrine of its Founder, at a very early stage. Now, this idea must be used by us to encourage once again the conception of a "historical Jesus" to be found by clearing away later "accretions and perversions" and then to be contrasted with the whole Christian tradition. In the last generation we promoted the construction of such a "historical Jesus" on liberal and humanitarian lines; we are now putting forward a new "historical Jesus" on Marxian, catastrophic, and revolutionary lines. The advantages of these constructions, which we intend to change every thirty years or so, are manifold. In the first place they all tend to direct men's devotion to something which does not exist, for each "historical Jesus" is unhistorical. The documents say what they say and cannot be added to; each new "historical Jesus" therefore has to be got out of them by suppression at one point and exaggeration at another, and by that sort of guessing (*brilliant* is the adjective we teach humans to apply to it) on which no one would risk ten shillings in ordinary life, but which is enough to produce a crop of new Napoleons, new Shakespeares, and new Swifts in every publisher's autumn list. In the second place, all such constructions place the importance of their "historical Jesus" in some peculiar theory He is supposed to have promulgated. He has to be a "great man" in the modern sense of the word—one standing at the terminus of some centrifugal and unbalanced line of thought—a crank vending a panacea. We thus distract men's minds from Who He is, and what He did. We first make Him solely a teacher, and then conceal the very substantial agreement between His teachings and those of all other great moral teachers. For humans must not be allowed to notice that all great moralists are sent by the Enemy, not to inform men, but to remind them, to restate the primeval moral platitudes against our continual concealment of them. We make the Sophists: He raises up a Socrates to answer them. Our third aim is, by these constructions, to destroy the devotional life. For the real presence of the Enemy, otherwise experienced by men in prayer and sacrament, we substitute a merely probable, remote, shadowy, and uncouth figure, one who spoke a strange language and died a long time ago. Such an object cannot in fact be worshipped. Instead of the Creator adored by its creature, you soon have merely a leader acclaimed by a partisan, and finally a distinguished character approved by a judicious historian. And fourthly, besides being unhistorical in the Jesus it depicts, religion of this kind is false to history in another sense. No nation, and few individuals, are really brought into the Enemy's camp by the historical study of the biography of Jesus, simply as biography. Indeed, materials for a full biography have been withheld from men. The earliest converts were converted by a single historical fact (the Resurrection) and a single theological doctrine (the Redemption) operating on a sense of sin which they already had—and sin, not against some new fancy-dress law produced as a novelty by a "great man," but against the old, platitudinous, universal moral law which they had been taught by their nurses and mothers. The "Gospels" come later, and were written, not to make Christians, but to edify Christians already made.

The Wisdom of Screwtape on the "Same Old Thing"

THE HORROR of the Same Old Thing is one of the most valuable passions we have produced in the human heart—an endless source of heresies in religion, folly in counsel, infidelity in marriage, and inconstancy in friendship. The humans live in time, and experience reality successively. To experience much of it, therefore, they must experience many different things; in other words, they must experience change. And since they need change, the Enemy (being a hedonist at heart) has made change pleasurable to them, just as He has made eating pleasurable. But since He does not wish them to make change, any more than eating, an end in itself, He has balanced the love of change in them by a love of permanence. He has contrived to gratify both tastes together in the very world He has made, by that union of change and permanence which we call Rhythm. He gives them the seasons, each season different yet every year the same, so that spring is always felt as a novelty yet always as the recurrence of an immemorial theme. He gives them in His Church a spiritual year; they change from a fast to a feast, but it is the same feast as before.

Now, just as we pick out and exaggerate the pleasure of eating to produce gluttony, so we pick out this natural pleasantness of change and twist it into a demand for absolute novelty. This demand is entirely our workmanship. If we neglect our duty, men will be not only contented but transported by the mixed novelty and familiarity of snowdrops *this* January, sunrise *this* morning, plum pudding *this* Christmas. Children, until we have taught them better, will be perfectly happy with a seasonal round of games in which conkers succeed hopscotch as regularly as autumn follows summer. Only by our incessant efforts is the demand for infinite, or unrhythmical, change kept up.

This demand is valuable in various ways. In the first place it diminishes pleasure while increasing desire. The pleasure of novelty is by its very nature more subject than any other to the law of diminishing returns. And continued novelty costs money, so that the desire for it spells avarice or unhappiness or both. And again, the more rapacious this desire, the sooner it must eat up all the innocent sources of pleasure and pass on to those the Enemy forbids. Thus by inflaming the horror of the Same Old Thing, we have recently made the Arts, for example, less dangerous to us than, perhaps, they have ever been, "lowbrow" and "highbrow" artists alike being now daily drawn into fresh, and still fresh, excesses of lasciviousness, unreason, cruelty, and pride. Finally, the desire for novelty is indispensable if we are to produce Fashions or Vogues.

The use of Fashions in thought is to distract the attention of men from their real dangers. We direct the fashionable outcry of each generation against those vices of which it is least in danger and fix its approval on the virtue nearest to that vice which we are trying to make endemic. The game is to have them all running about with fire extinguishers whenever there is a flood, and all crowding to that side of the boat which is already nearly gunwale under. Thus we make it fashionable to expose the dangers of enthusiasm at the very moment when they are all really becoming worldly and lukewarm; a century later, when we are really making them all Byronic and drunk with emotion, the fashionable outcry is directed against the dangers of the mere "understanding." Cruel ages are put on their guard against Sentimentality, feckless and idle ones against Respectability, lecherous ones against Puritanism; and whenever all men are really hastening to be slaves or tyrants we make Liberalism the prime bogey.

But the greatest triumph of all is to elevate this horror of the Same Old Thing into a philosophy so that nonsense in the intellect may reinforce corruption in the will. It is here that the general Evolutionary or Historical character of modern European thought (partly our work) comes in so usefully. The Enemy loves platitudes. Of a proposed course of action He wants men, so far as I can see, to ask very simple questions: Is it righteous? Is it prudent? Is it possible? Now, if we can keep men asking: "Is it in accordance with the general movement of our time? Is it progressive or reactionary? Is this the way that History is going?" they will neglect the relevant questions. And the questions they *do* ask are, of course, unanswerable; for they do not know the future, and what the future will be depends very largely on just those choices which they now invoke the future to help them to make. As a result, while their minds are buzzing in this vacuum, we have the better chance to slip in and bend them to the action *we* have decided on. And great work has already been done. Once they knew that some changes were for the better, and others for the worse, and others again indifferent. We have largely removed this knowledge. For the descriptive adjective "unchanged" we have substituted the emotional adjective "stagnant." We have trained them to think of the future as a promised land which favoured heroes attain—not as something which everyone reaches at the rate of sixty minutes an hour, whatever he does, whoever he is.

Your affectionate uncle

SCREWTAPE

The Wisdom of Screwtape on the Appetite for Heaven

THE TRUTH is that the Enemy, having oddly destined these mere animals to life in His own eternal world, has guarded them pretty effectively from the danger of feeling at home anywhere else. That is why we must often wish long life to our patients; seventy years is not a day too much for the difficult task of unravelling their souls from Heaven and building up a firm attachment to the Earth. While they are young we find them always shooting off at a tangent. Even if we contrive to keep them ignorant of explicit religion, the incalculable winds of fantasy and music and poetry—the mere face of a girl, the song of a bird, or the sight of a horizon—are always blowing our whole structure away. They *will* not apply themselves steadily to worldly advancement, prudent connections, and the policy of safety first. So inveterate is their appetite for Heaven, that our best method, at this stage, of attaching them to Earth is to make them believe that Earth can be turned into Heaven at some future date by politics or eugenics or "science" or psychology or what not. Real worldiness is a work of time—assisted, of course, by pride, for we teach them to describe the creeping death as Good Sense or Maturity or Experience. *Experience*, in the peculiar sense we teach them to give it, is, by the bye, a most useful word. A great human philosopher nearly let our secret out when he said that where Virtue is concerned "Experience is the mother of illusion"; but thanks to a change in Fashion, and also, of course, to the Historical Point of View, we have largely rendered his book innocuous.

The Wisdom of Screwtape on the Moment of Death

As HE SAW YOU, he also saw Them. I know how it was. You reeled back dizzy and blinded, more hurt by them than he had ever been by bombs. The degradation of it!—that this thing of earth and slime could stand upright and converse with spirits before whom you, a spirit, could only cower. Perhaps you had hoped that the awe and strangeness of it would dash his joy. But that is the cursed thing; the gods are strange to mortal eyes, and yet they are not strange. He had no faintest conception till that very hour of how they would look, and even doubted their existence. But when he saw them he knew that he had always known them and realised what part each one of them had played at many an hour in his life when he had supposed himself alone, so that now he could say to them, one by one, not "Who *are* you?" but "So it was *you* all the time." All that they were and said at this meeting woke memories. The dim consciousness of friends about him which had haunted his solitudes from infancy was now at last explained; that central music in every pure experience which had always just evaded memory was now at last recovered. Recognition made him free of their company almost before the limbs of his corpse became quiet. Only you were left outside.

He saw not only Them; he saw Him. This animal, this thing begotten in a bed, could look on Him. What is blinding, suffocating fire to you is now cool light to him, is clarity itself, and wears the form of a Man. You would like, if you could, to interpret the patient's prostration in the Presence, his self-abhorrence and utter knowledge of his sins (yes, Wormwood, a clearer knowledge even than yours) on the analogy of your own choking and paralysing sensations when you encounter the deadly air that breathes from the heart of Heaven. But it's all nonsense. Pains he may still have to encounter, but they *embrace* those pains. They would not barter them for any earthly pleasure. All the delights of sense or heart or intellect with which you could once have tempted him, even the delights of virtue itself, now seem to him in comparison but as the half-nauseous attractions of a raddled harlot would seem to a man who hears that his true beloved whom he has loved all his life and whom he had believed to be dead is alive and even now at his door. He is caught up into that world where pain and pleasure take on transfinite values and where all our arithmetic is dismayed. Once more, the inexplicable meets us. Next to the curse of useless tempters like yourself, the greatest curse upon us is the failure of our Intelligence Department. If we could only find out what He is really up to! Alas, alas, that knowledge, in itself so hateful and mawkish a thing, should yet be necessary for Power! Sometimes I am almost in despair. All that sutains me is the conviction that our Realism, our rejection (in the face of all temptations) of all silly nonsense and claptrap, *must* win in the end. Meanwhile, I have you to settle with. Most truly do I sign myself

Your increasingly and ravenously
affectionate uncle
Screwtape

The Wisdom of Screwtape on Democracy

It is our function to encourage the behaviour, the manners, the whole attitude of mind, which democracies naturally like and enjoy, because these are the very things which, if unchecked, will destroy democracy. You would almost wonder that even humans don't see it themselves. Even if they don't read Aristotle (that would be undemocratic) you would have thought the French Revolution would have taught them that the behaviour aristocrats naturally like is not the behaviour that preserves aristocracy. They might then have applied the same principle to all forms of government.

But I would not end on that note. I would not—Hell forbid! encourage in your own minds that delusion which you must carefully foster in the minds of your human victims. I mean the delusion that the fate of nations is *in itself* more important than that of individual souls. The overthrow of free peoples and the multiplication of slave states are for us a means (besides, of course, being fun); but the real end is the destruction of individuals. For only individuals can be saved or damned, can become sons of the Enemy or food for us. The ultimate value, for us, of any revolution, war, or famine lies in the individual anguish, treachery, hatred, rage, and despair which it may produce. *I'm as good as you* is a useful means for the destruction of democratic societies. But it has a far deeper value as an end in itself, as a state of mind which, necessarily excluding humility, charity, contentment, and all the pleasures of gratitude or admiration, turns a human being away from almost every road which might finally lead him to Heaven.

Marriage

"I don't think," he said, "that 'joining us' would mean, at the moment, coming to live at St. Anne's, specially in the case of a married woman. Unless old Mark got really interested and came himself—"

"That is quite out of the question," said Jane.

("He doesn't know Mark," she thought.)

"Anyway," continued Denniston, "that is hardly the real point at the moment. Would he object to your joining—putting yourself under the Head's orders and making the promises and all that?"

"Would he object?" asked Jane. "What on earth would it have to do with him?"

"Well," said Denniston, hesitating a little, "the Head— or the authorities he obeys—have rather old-fashioned notions. He wouldn't like a married woman to come in, if it could be avoided, without her husband's—without consulting—"

"Do you mean I'm to ask Mark's *permission?*" said Jane with a strained little laugh. The resentment which had been rising and ebbing, but rising each time a little more than it ebbed, for several minutes, had now overflowed. All this talk of promises and obedience to an unknown Mr. Fisher-King had already repelled her. But the idea of this same person sending her back to get Mark's permission—as if she were a child asking leave to go to a party—was the climax. For a moment she looked on Mr. Denniston with real dislike. She saw him, and Mark, and the Fisher-King man and this preposterous Indian fakir simply as Men—complacent, patriarchal figures making arrangements for women as if women were children or bartering them like cattle. ("And so the king promised that if anyone killed the dragon he would *give* him his daughter in marriage.") She was very angry.

Marriage

"IT WAS NOT his fault," she said at last. "I suppose our marriage was just a mistake."

The Director said nothing.

"What would you—what would the people you are talking of—say about a case like that?"

"I will tell you if you really want to know," said the Director.

"Please," said Jane reluctantly.

"They would say," he answered, "that you do not fail in obedience through lack of love, but have lost love because you never attempted obedience."

Something in Jane that would normally have reacted to such a remark with anger or laughter was banished to a remote distance (where she could still, but only just, hear its voice) by the fact that the word Obedience—but certainly not obedience to Mark—came over her, in that room and in that presence, like a strange oriental perfume, perilous, seductive, and ambiguous . . .

"Stop it!" said the Director, sharply.

Jane stared at him, open mouthed. There were a few moments of silence during which the exotic fragrance faded away.

"You were saying, my dear?" resumed the Director.

"I thought love meant equality," she said, "and free companionship."

"Ah, equality!" said the Director. "We must talk of that some other time. Yes, we must all be guarded by equal rights from one another's greed, because we are fallen. Just as we must all wear clothes for the same reason. But the naked body should be there underneath the clothes, ripening for the day when we shall need them no longer. Equality is not the deepest thing, you know."

"I always thought that was just what it was. I thought it was in their souls that people were equal."

"You were mistaken," said he gravely. "That is the last place where they are equal. Equality before the law, equality of incomes—that is very well. Equality guards life; it doesn't make it. It is medicine, not food. You might as well try to warm yourself with a blue-book."

"But surely in marriage . . . ?"

"Worse and worse," said the Director. "Courtship knows nothing of it; nor does fruition. What has free companionship to do with that? Those who are enjoying something, or suffering something together, are companions. Those who enjoy or suffer one another, are not. Do you not know how bashful friendship is? Friends—comrades—do not look *at* each other. Friendship would be ashamed . . ."

"I thought," said Jane and stopped.

"I see," said the Director. "It is not your fault. They never warned you. No one has ever told you that obedience—humility—is an erotic necessity. You are putting equality just where it ought not to be."

Maturity

"I WAS YOUNG yesterday," she said. "When I laughed at you. Now I know that the people in your world do not like to be laughed at."

"You say you were young?"

"Yes."

"Are you not young to-day also?"

She appeared to be thinking for a few moments, so intently that the flowers dropped, unregarded, from her hand.

"I see it now," she said presently. "It is very strange to say one is young at the moment one is speaking. But to-morrow I shall be older. And then I shall say I was young to-day. You are quite right. This is great wisdom you are bringing, O Piebald Man."

"What do you mean?"

"This looking backward and forward along the line and seeing how a day has one appearance as it comes to you, and another when you are in it, and a third when it has gone past. Like the waves."

"But you are very little older than yesterday."

"How do you know that?"

"I mean," said Ransom, "a night is not a very long time."

She thought again, and then spoke suddenly, her face lightening. "I see it now," she said. "You think times have lengths. A night is always a night whatever you do in it, as from this tree to that is always so many paces whether you take them quickly or slowly. I suppose that is true in a way. But the waves do not always come at equal distances. I see that you come from a wise world . . . if this is wise. I have never done it before—stepping out of life into the Along-side and looking at oneself living as if one were not alive. Do they all do that in your world, Piebald?"

"What do you know about other worlds?" said Ransom.

"I know this. Beyond the roof it is all Deep Heaven, the high place. And the low is not really spread out as it seems to be" (here she indicated the whole landscape) "but is rolled up into little balls: little lumps of the low swimming in the high. And the oldest and greatest of them have on them that which we have never seen nor heard and cannot at all understand. But on the younger Maleldil has made to grow the things like us, that breathe and breed."

"How have you found all this out? Your roof is so dense that your people cannot see through into Deep Heaven and look at the other worlds."

Up till now her face had been grave. At this point she

clapped her hands and a smile such as Ransom had never seen changed her. One does not see that smile here except in children, but there was nothing of the child about it there.

"Oh, I see it," she said. "I am older now. Your world has no roof. You look right out into the high place and see the great dance with your own eyes. You live always in that terror and that delight, and what we must only believe you can behold. Is not this a wonderful invention of Maleldil's? When I was young I could imagine no beauty but this of our own world. But He can think of all, and all different."

"That is one of the things that is bewildering me," said Ransom. "That you are not different. You are shaped like the women of my own kind. I had not expected that. I have been in one other world beside my own. But the creatures there are not at all like you and me."

"What is bewildering about it?"

"I do not see why different worlds should bring forth like creatures. Do different trees bring forth like fruit?"

"But that other world was older than yours," she said.

"How do you know that?" asked Ransom in amazement.

"Maleldil is telling me," answered the woman. And as she spoke the landscape had become different, though with a difference none of the senses would identify. The light was dim, the air gentle, and all Ransom's body was bathed in bliss, but the garden world where he stood seemed to be packed quite full, and as if an unendurable pressure had been laid upon his shoulders, his legs failed him and he half sank, half fell, into a sitting position.

"It all comes into my mind now," she continued. "I see the big furry creatures, and the white giants—what is it you call them?—the Sorns, and the blue rivers. Oh, what a strong pleasure it would be to see them with my outward eyes, to touch them, and the stronger because there are no more of that kind to come. It is only in the ancient worlds they linger yet."

"Why?" said Ransom in a whisper, looking up at her.

"You must know that better than I," she said. "For was it not in your own world that all this happened?"

"All what?"

"I thought it would be you who would tell me of it," said the woman, now in her turn bewildered.

"What are you talking about?" said Ransom.

"I mean," said she, "that in your world Maleldil first took Himself this form, the form of your race and mine."

A Mythological God and His God

THE CROWD AND THE DANCE round Aslan (for it had become a dance once more) grew so thick and rapid that Lucy was confused. She never saw where certain other people came from who were soon capering about among the trees. One was a youth, dressed only in a fawn-skin, with vine-leaves wreathed in his curly hair. His face would have been almost too pretty for a boy's, if it had not looked so extremely wild. You felt, as Edmund said when he saw him a few days later, "There's a chap who might do anything—absolutely anything." He seemed to have a great many names—Bromios, Bassareus, and the Ram, were three of them. There were a lot of girls with him, as wild as he. There was even, unexpectedly, someone on a donkey. And everybody was laughing: and everybody was shouting out, "Euan, euan, eu-oi-oi-oi."

"Is it a Romp, Aslan?" cried the youth. And apparently it was. But nearly everyone seemed to have a different idea as to what they were playing. It may have been Tig, but Lucy never discovered who was It. It was rather like Blind Man's

Buff, only everyone behaved as if he was blindfolded. It was not unlike Hunt the Slipper, but the slipper was never found. What made it more complicated was that the man on the donkey, who was old and enormously fat, began calling out at once. "Refreshments! Time for refreshments," and falling off his donkey and being bundled on to it again by the others, while the donkey was under the impression that the whole thing was a circus, and tried to give a display of walking on its hind legs. And all the time there were more and more vineleaves everywhere! And soon not only leaves but vines. They were climbing up everything. They were running up the legs of the tree people and circling round their necks. Lucy put up her hands to push back her hair and found she was pushing back vine branches. The donkey was a mass of them. His tail was completely entangled and something dark was nodding between his ears. Lucy looked again and saw it was a bunch of grapes. After that it was mostly grapes—overhead and underfoot and all around.

"Refreshments! Refreshments," roared the old man. Everyone began eating, and whatever hot-houses your people may have, you have never tasted such grapes. Really good grapes, firm and tight on the outside, but bursting into cool sweetness when you put them into your mouth, were one of the things the girls had never had quite enough of before. Here, there were more than anyone could possibly want, and no table-manners at all. One saw sticky and stained fingers everywhere, and, though mouths were full the laughter never ceased nor the yodelling cries of *Euan, euan, eu-oi-oi-oi-oi*, till all of a sudden everyone felt at the same moment that the game (whatever it was), and the feast, ought to be over, and everyone flopped down breathless on the ground and turned his face to Aslan to hear what he would say next.

At that moment the sun was just rising and Lucy remembered something and whispered to Susan,

"I say, Su, I know who they are."

"Who?"

"The boy with the wild face is Bacchus and the old one on the donkey is Silenus. Don't you remember Mr. Tumnus telling us about them long ago?"

"Yes, of course. But I say, Lu——"

"What?"

"I wouldn't have felt very safe with Bacchus and all his wild girls if we'd met them without Aslan."

"I should think not," said Lucy.

Mythology

WITH DEEP WONDER he thought to himself, "My eyes have seen Mars and Venus. I have seen Ares and Aphrodite." He asked them how they were known to the old poets of Tellus. When and from whom had the children of Adam learned that Ares was a man of war and that Aphrodite rose from the sea foam? Earth has been besieged, an enemy-occupied territory, since before history began. The gods have had no commerce there. How then do we know of them? It comes, they told him, a long way round and through many stages. There is an environment of minds as well as of space. The universe is one—a spider's web wherein each mind lives along every line, a vast whispering gallery where (save for the direct action of Maleldil) though no news travels unchanged yet no secret can be rigorously kept. In the mind of the fallen Archon under whom our planet groans, the memory of Deep Heaven and the gods with whom he once consorted is still alive. Nay, in the very matter of our world, the traces of the celestial commonwealth are not quite lost. Memory passes through the womb and hovers in the air. The Muse is a real thing. A faint breath, as Virgil says, reaches even the late generations. Our mythology is based on a solider reality than we dream: but it is also at an almost infinite distance from that base. And when they told him this, Ransom at last understood why mythology was what it was—gleams of celestial strength and beauty falling on a jungle of filth and imbecility. His cheeks burned on behalf of our race when he looked on the true Mars and Venus and remembered the follies that have been talked of them on Earth. Then a doubt struck him.

"But do I see you as you really are?" he asked.

"Only Maleldil sees any creature as it really is," said Mars.

"How do you see one another?" asked Ransom.

"There are no holding places in your mind for an answer to that."

"Am I then seeing only an appearance? Is it not real at all?"

"You see only an appearance, small one. You have never seen more than an appearance of anything—not of Arbol, nor of a stone, nor of your own body. This appearance is as true as what you see of those."

"But . . . there were those other appearances."

"No. There was only the failure of appearance."

"I don't understand," said Ransom. "Were all those other things—the wheels and the eyes—more real than this or less?"

"There is no meaning in your question," said Mars. "You can see a stone, if it is a fit distance from you and if you and it are moving at speeds not too different. But if one throws the stone at your eye, what then is the appearance?"

"I should feel pain and perhaps see splintered light," said Ransom. "But I don't know that I should call that an appearance of the stone."

"Yet it would be the true operation of the stone. And there is your question answered. We are now at the right distance from you."

"And were you nearer in what I first saw?"

"I do not mean that kind of distance."

"And then," said Ransom, still pondering, "there is what I had thought was your wonted appearance—the very faint light, Oyarsa, as I used to see it in your own world. What of that?"

"That is enough appearance for us to speak to you by. No more was needed between us: no more is needed now. It is to honour the King that we would now appear more. That light is the overflow or echo into the world of your senses of vehicles made for appearance to one enother and to the greater eldila."

Paganism

A CLICHÉ CAME OUT OF ITS CAGE

1

You said "The world is going back to Paganism." Oh bright
Vision! I saw our dynasty in the bar of the House
Spill from their tumblers a libation to the Erinyes,
And Leavis with Lord Russell wreathed in flowers, heralded
    with flutes,
Leading white bulls to the cathedral of the solemn Muses
To pay where due the glory of their latest theorem.
Hestia's fire in every flat, rekindled, burned before
The Lardergods. Unmarried daughters with obedient hands
Tended it. By the hearth the white-arm'd venerable mother
Domum servabat, lanam faciebat. Duly at the hour
Of sacrifice their brothers came, silent, corrected, grave
Before their elders; on their downy cheeks easily the blush
Arose (it is the mark of freemen's children) as they trooped,
Gleaming with oil, demurely home from the palaestra or the
    dance.
Walk carefully, do not wake the envy of the happy gods,
Shun Hubris. The middle of the road, the middle sort of
    men,
Are best. Aidos surpasses gold. Reverence for the aged
Is wholesome as seasonable rain, and for a man to die
Defending the city in battle is a harmonious thing.
Thus with magistral hand the Puritan Sophrosune
Cooled and schooled and tempered our uneasy motions;
Heathendom came again, the circumspection and the holy
    fears . . .
You said it. Did you mean it? Oh inordinate liar, stop.

2

Or did you mean another kind of heathenry?
Think, then, that under heaven-roof the little disc of the
    earth,
Fortified Midgard, lies encircled by the ravening Worm.
Over its icy bastions faces of giant and troll
Look in, ready to invade it. The Wolf, admittedly, is bound;
But the bond will break, the Beast run free. The weary gods,
Scarred with old wounds, the one-eyed Odin, Tyr who has
    lost a hand,
Will limp to their stations for the last defence. Make it your
    hope
To be counted worthy on that day to stand beside them;
For the end of man is to partake of their defeat and die
His second, final death in good company. The stupid,
    strong
Unteachable monsters are certain to be victorious at last,
And every man of decent blood is on the losing side.
Take as your model the tall women with yellow hair in
    plaits
Who walked back into burning houses to die with men,
Or him who as the death spear entered into his vitals
Made critical comments on its workmanship and aim.
Are these the Pagans you spoke of? Know your betters and
    crouch, dogs;
You that have Vichy-water in your veins and worship the
    event,
Your goddess History (whom your fathers called the strum-
    pet Fortune).

Fairy Tales *

I HAVE CALLED this a fairy-tale in the hope that no one who
dislikes fantasy may be misled by the first two chapters into
reading further, and then complain of his disappointment.
If you ask why—intending to write about magicians, devils,
pantomime animals, and planetary angels—I nevertheless
begin with such hum-drum scenes and persons, I reply that
I am following the traditional fairy-tale. We do not always
notice its method, because the cottages, castles, woodcut-
ters, and petty kings with which a fairy-tale opens have become for us as remote as the witches and ogres to which it
proceeds. But they were not remote at all to the men who
made and first enjoyed the stories. They were, indeed, more
realistic and commonplace than Bracton College is to me:
for many German peasants had actually met cruel stepmoth-
ers, whereas I have never, in any university, come across a
college like Bracton. This is a "tall story" about devilry,
though it has behind it a serious "point" which I have tried
to make in my *Abolition of Man*. In the story, the outer rim
of that devilry had to be shown touching the life of some
ordinary and respectable profession. I selected my own
profession, not, of course, because I think fellows of col-
leges more likely to be thus corrupted than anyone else, but
because my own is the only profession I know well enough
to write about. A very small university is imagined because
that has certain conveniences for fiction. Edgestow has no
resemblance, save for its smallness, to Durham—a university with which the only connection I have had was entirely
pleasant.

*From *That Hideous Strength*.

Meeting with a Hross

THERE WAS NO SOUND of pursuit. Ransom dropped down on his stomach and drank, cursing a world where *cold* water appeared to be unobtainable. Then he lay still to listen and to recover his breath. His eyes were upon the blue water. It was agitated. Circles shuddered and bubbles danced ten yards away from his face. Suddenly the water heaved and a round, shining, black thing like a cannon-ball came into sight. Then he saw eyes and mouth—a puffing mouth bearded with bubbles. More of the thing came up out of the water. It was gleaming black. Finally it splashed and wallowed to the shore and rose, steaming, on its hind legs—six or seven feet high and too thin for its height, like everything in Malacandra. It had a coat of thick black hair, lucid as seal-skin, very short legs with webbed feet, a broad beaver-like or fish-like tail, strong forelimbs with webbed claws or fingers, and some complication half-way up the belly which Ransom took to be its genitals. It was something like a penguin, something like an otter, something like a seal; the slenderness and flexibility of the body suggested a giant stoat. The great round head, heavily whiskered, was mainly responsible for the suggestion of seal; but it was higher in the forehead than a seal's and the mouth was smaller.

There comes a point at which the actions of fear and precaution are purely conventional, no longer felt as terror or hope by the fugitive. Ransom lay perfectly still, pressing his body as well down into the weed as he could, in obedience to a wholly theoretical idea that he might thus pass unobserved. He felt little emotion. He noted in a dry, objective way that this was apparently to be the end of his story—caught between a *sorn* from the land and a big black animal from the water. He had, it is true, a vague notion that the jaws and mouth of the beast were not those of a carnivore; but he knew that he was too ignorant of zoology to do more than guess.

Then something happened which completely altered his state of mind. The creature, which was still steaming and shaking itself on the back and had obviously not seen him, opened its mouth and began to make noises. This in itself was not remarkable; but a lifetime of linguistic study assured Ransom almost at once that these were articulate noises. The creature was *talking*. It had a language. If you are not yourself a philologist, I am afraid you must take on trust the prodigious emotional consequences of this realization in Ransom's mind. A new world he had already seen—but a new, an extra-terrestrial, a non-human language was a different matter. Somehow he had not thought of this in connection with the *sorns;* now, it flashed upon him like a revelation. The love of knowledge is a kind of madness. In the fraction of a second which it took Ransom to decide that the creature was really talking, and while he still knew that he might be facing instant death, his imagination had leaped over every fear and hope and probability of his situation to follow the dazzling project of making a Malacandrian grammar. *An Introduction to the Malacandrian language—The Lunar verb—A Concise Martian-English Dictionary* . . . the titles flitted through his mind. And what might one not discover from the speech of a non-human race? The very form of language itself, the principle behind all possible languages, might fall into his hands. Unconsciously he raised himself on his elbow and stared at the black beast. It became silent. The huge bullet head swung round and lustrous amber eyes fixed him. There was no wind on the lake or in the wood. Minute after minute in utter silence the representatives of two so far-divided species stared each into the other's face.

Ransom rose to his knees. The creature leaped back,

watching him intently, and they became motionless again. Then it came a pace nearer, and Ransom jumped up and retreated, but not far; curiosity held him. He summoned up his courage and advanced, holding out his hand; the beast misunderstood the gesture. It backed into the shallows of the lake and he could see the muscles tightened under its sleek pelt, ready for sudden movement. But there it stopped; it, too, was in the grip of curiosity. Neither dared let the other approach, yet each repeatedly felt the impulse to do so himself, and yielded to it. It was foolish, frightening, ecstatic and unbearable all in one moment. It was more than curiosity. It was like a courtship—like the meeting of the first man and the first woman in the world; it was like something beyond that; so natural is the contact of sexes, so limited the strangeness, so shallow the reticence, so mild the repugnance to be overcome, compared with the first tingling intercourse of two different, but rational, species.

Meeting with a Sorn

IT WAS SITTING on its long, wedged-shaped buttocks with its feet drawn close up to it. A man in the same posture would have rested his chin on his knees, but the *sorn's* legs were too long for that. Its knees rose high above its shoulders on each side of its head—grotesquely suggestive of huge ears—and the head, down between them, rested its chin on the protruding breast. The creature seemed to have either a double chin or a beard; Ransom could not make out which in the firelight. It was mainly white or cream in colour and seemed to be clothed down to the ankles in some soft substance that reflected the light. On the long fragile shanks, where the creature was closest to him, he saw that this was some natural kind of coat. It was not like fur but more like feathers. In fact it was almost exactly like feathers. The whole animal, seen at close quarters, was less terrifying than he had expected, and even a little smaller. The face, it was true, took a good deal of getting used to—it was too long, too solemn and too colourless, and it was much more unpleasantly like a human face than any inhuman creature's face ought to be. Its eyes, like those of all very large creatures, seemed too small for it. But it was more grotesque than horrible. A new conception of the *sorns* began to arise in his mind: the ideas of "giant" and "ghost" receded behind those of "goblin" and "gawk."

"Perhaps you are hungry, Small One," it said.

Ransom was. The *sorn* rose with strange spidery movements and began going to and fro about the cave, attended by its thin goblin shadow. It brought him the usual vegetable foods of Malacandra, and strong drink, with the very welcome addition of a smooth brown substance which revealed itself to nose, eye and palate, in defiance of all probability, as cheese. Ransom asked what it was.

The *sorn* began to explain painfully how the female of some animals secreted a fluid for the nourishment of its young, and would have gone on to describe the whole process of milking and cheesemaking, if Ransom had not interrupted it.

"Yes, yes," he said. "We do the same on Earth. What is the beast you use?"

"It is a yellow beast with a long neck. It feeds on the forests that grow in the *handramit*. The young ones of our people who are not yet fit for much else drive the beasts down there in the mornings and follow them while they feed; then before night they drive them back and put them in the caves."

For a moment Ransom found something reassuring in the thought that the *sorns* were shepherds. Then he remembered that the Cyclops in Homer plied the same trade.

Meeting with a Pfifltrigg

IT WAS HAIRLESS like a man's or a *sorn's*. It was long and pointed like a shrew's, yellow and shabby-looking, and so low in the forehead that but for the heavy development of the head at the back and behind the ears (like a bag-wig) it could not have been that of an intelligent creature. A moment later the whole of the thing came into view with a startling jump. Ransom guessed that it was a *pfifltrigg*—and was glad that he had not met one of this third race on his first arrival in Malacandra. It was much more insect-like or reptilian than anything he had yet seen. Its build was distinctly that of a frog, and at first Ransom thought it was resting, frog-like, on its "hands." Then he noticed that that part of its fore-limbs on which it was supported was really, in human terms, rather an elbow than a hand. It was broad and padded and clearly made to be walked on; but upwards from it, at an angle of about forty-five degrees, went the true fore-arms—thin, strong fore-arms, ending in enormous, sensitive, many-fingered hands. He realized that for all manual work from mining to cutting cameos this creature had the advantage of being able to work with its full strength from a supported elbow. The insect-like effect was due to the speed and jerkiness of its movements and to the fact that it could swivel its head almost all the way round like a mantis; and it was increased by a kind of dry, rasping, jingling quality in the noise of its moving. It was rather like a grasshopper, rather like one of Arthur Rackham's dwarfs, rather like a frog, and rather like a little, old taxidermist whom Ransom knew in London.

"I come from another world," began Ransom.

"I know, I know," said the creature in a quick, twittering,

rather impatient voice. "Come here, behind the stone. This way, this way. Oyarsa's orders. Very busy. Must begin at once. Stand there."

Ransom found himself on the other side of the monolith, staring at a picture which was still in process of completion. The ground was liberally strewn with chips and the air was full of dust.

"There," said the creature. "Stand still. Don't look at me. Look over there."

For a moment Ransom did not quite understand what was expected of him; then, as he saw the *pfifltrigg* glancing to and fro at him and at the stone with the unmistakable glance of artist from model to work which is the same in all worlds, he realized and almost laughed. He was standing for his portrait! From his position he could see that the creature was cutting the stone as if it were cheese and the swiftness of its movements almost baffled his eyes, but he could get no impression of the work done, though he could study the *pfifltrigg*. He saw that the jingling and metallic noise was due to the number of small instruments which it carried about its body. Sometimes, with an exclamation of annoyance, it would throw down the tool it was working with and select one of these; but the majority of those in immediate use it kept in its mouth. He realized also that this was an animal artificially clothed like himself, in some bright scaly substance which appeared richly decorated though coated in dust. It had folds of furry clothing about its throat like a comforter, and its eyes were protected by dark bulging goggles. Rings and chains of a bright metal—not gold, he thought—adorned its limbs and neck. All the time it was working it kept up a sort of hissing whisper to itself; and when it was excited—which it usually was—the end of its nose wrinkled like a rabbit's. At last it gave another startling leap, landed ten yards away from its work, and said:

"Yes, yes. Not so good as I hoped. Do better another time. Leave it now. Come and see yourself."

Ransom obeyed. He saw a picture of the planets, not now arranged to make a map of the solar system, but advancing in a single procession towards the spectator, and all, save one, bearing its fiery charioteer. Below lay Malacandra and there, to his surprise, was a very tolerable picture of the space-ship. Beside it stood three figures for all of which Ransom had apparently been the model. He recoiled from them in disgust. Even allowing for the strangeness of the subject from a Malacandrian point of view and for the stylization of their art, still, he thought, the creature might have made a better attempt at the human form than these stocklike dummies, almost as thick as they were tall, and sprouting about the head and neck into something that looked like fungus.

He hedged. "I expect it is like me as I look to your people," he said. "It is not how they would draw me in my own world."

"No," said the *pfifltrigg*. "I do not mean it to be too like. Too like, and they will not believe it—those who are born after." He added a good deal more which was difficult to understand; but while he was speaking it dawned upon Ransom that the odious figures were intended as an *idealization* of humanity.

Bereavement

AS THE RUIN FALLS

All this is flashy rhetoric about loving you.
I never had a selfless thought since I was born.
I am mercenary and self-seeking through and through:
I want God, you, all friends, merely to serve my turn.

Peace, re-assurance, pleasure, are the goals I seek,
I cannot crawl one inch outside my proper skin:
I talk of love—a scholar's parrot may talk Greek—
But, self-imprisoned, always end where I begin.

Only that now you have taught me (but how late) my lack.
I see the chasm. And everything you are was making
My heart into a bridge by which I might get back
From exile, and grow man. And now the bridge is breaking

For this I bless you as the ruin falls. The pains
You give me are more precious than all other gains.

Death in Wartime

DEATH IN BATTLE

Open the gates for me,
Open the gates of the peaceful castle, rosy in the West,
In the sweet dim Isle of Apples over the wide sea's breast,
Open the gates for me!

Sorely pressed have I been
And driven and hurt beyond bearing this summer day,
But the heat and the pain together suddenly fall away,
All's cool and green.

But a moment agone,
Among men cursing in fight and toiling, blinded I fought,
But the labour passed on a sudden even as a passing
    thought,
And now—alone!

Ah, to be ever alone,
In flowery valleys among the mountains and silent wastes
    untrod,
In the dewy upland places, in the garden of God,
This would atone!

I shall not see
The brutal, crowded faces around me, that in their toil have
    grown
Into the the faces of devils—yea, even as my own—
When I find thee,

O Country of Dreams!
Beyond the tide of the ocean, hidden and sunk away,

Out of the sound of battles, near to the end of day,
Full of dim woods and streams.

The Inner Circle

"Yes," said Curry, "it will take the hell of a time. Probably go on after dinner. We shall have all the obstructionists wasting time as hard as they can. But luckily that's the worst they can do."

You would never have guessed from the tone of Studdock's reply what intense pleasure he derived from Curry's use of the pronoun "we." So very recently he had been an outsider, watching the proceedings of what he then called "Curry and his gang" with awe and with little understanding, and making at College meetings short, nervous speeches which never influenced the course of events. Now he was inside and "Curry and his gang" had become "we" or "the Progressive Element in College." It had all happened quite suddenly and was still sweet in the mouth.

"You think it'll go through, then?" said Studdock.

"Sure to," said Curry. "We've got the Warden, and the Bursar, and all the chemical and bio-chemical people for a start. I've tackled Pelham and Ted and they're sound. I've made Sancho believe that he sees the point and that he's in favour of it. Bill the Blizzard will probably do something pretty devastating but he's bound to side with us if it comes to a vote. Besides, I haven't yet told you. Dick's going to be there. He came up in time for dinner last night and got busy at once."

Studdock's mind darted hither and thither in search of some safe way to conceal the fact that he did not know who Dick was. In the nick of time he remembered a very obscure colleague whose Christian name was Richard.

"Telford?" said Studdock in a puzzled voice. He knew very well that Telford could not be the Dick that Curry meant and therefore threw a slightly whimsical and ironical tone into his question.

"Good Lord! Telford!!" said Curry with a laugh. "No. I mean Lord Feverstone—Dick Devine as he used to be."

"I *was* a little baffled by the idea of Telford," said Studdock, joining in the laugh. "I'm glad Feverstone is coming. I've never met him, you know."

"Oh, but you must," said Curry. "Look here, come and dine in my rooms tonight. I've asked him."

From Lizard to Steed

"HAVE I YOUR PERMISSION?" said the Angel to the Ghost.

"I know it will kill me."

"It won't. But supposing it did?"

"You're right. It would be better to be dead than to live with this creature."

"Then I may?"

"Damn and blast you! Go on can't you? Get it over. Do what you like," bellowed the Ghost: but ended, whimpering, "God help me. God help me."

Next moment the Ghost gave a scream of agony such as I never heard on Earth. The Burning One closed his crimson grip on the reptile: twisted it, while it bit and writhed, and then flung it, broken backed, on the turf.

"Ow! That's done for me," gasped the Ghost, reeling backwards.

For a moment I could make out nothing distinctly. Then I saw, between me and the nearest bush, unmistakably solid but growing every moment solider, the upper arm and the shoulder of a man. Then, brighter still and stronger, the legs and hands. The neck and golden head materialised while I watched, and if my attention had not wavered I should have seen the actual completing of a man—an immense man, naked, not much smaller than the Angel. What distracted me was the fact that at the same moment something seemed to be happening to the Lizard. At first I thought the operation had failed. So far from dying, the creature was still struggling and even growing bigger as it struggled. And as it grew it changed. Its hinder parts grew rounder. The tail, still flickering, became a tail of hair that flickered between huge and glossy buttocks. Suddenly I started back, rubbing my eyes. What stood before me was the greatest stallion I have ever seen, silvery white but with mane and tail of gold. It was smooth and shining, rippled with swells of flesh and muscle, whinnying and stamping with its hoofs. At each stamp the land shook and the trees dindled.

The new-made man turned and clapped the new horse's neck. It nosed his bright body. Horse and master breathed each into the other's nostrils. The man turned from it, flung himself at the feet of the Burning One, and embraced them. When he rose I thought his face shone with tears, but it may have been only the liquid love and brightness (one cannot distinguish them in that country) which flowed from him. I had not long to think about it. In joyous haste the young man leaped upon the horse's back. Turning in his seat he waved a farewell, then nudged the stallion with his heels. They were off before I well knew what was happening. There was riding if you like! I came out as quickly as I could from among the bushes to follow them with my eyes; but already they were only like a shooting star far off on the green plain, and soon among the foothills of the mountains. Then, still like a star, I saw them winding up, scaling what seemed impossible steeps, and quicker every moment, till near the dim brow of the landscape, so high that I must

strain my neck to see them, they vanished, bright themselves, into the rose-brightness of that everlasting morning.

While I still watched, I noticed that the whole plain and
forest were shaking with a sound which in our world would
be too large to hear, but there I could take it with joy. I
knew it was not the Solid People who were singing. It was
the voice of that earth, those woods and those waters. A
strange archaic, inorganic noise, that came from all directions at once. The Nature or Arch-nature of that land rejoiced to have been once more ridden, and therefore
consummated, in the person of the horse. It sang,

The Master says to our master, Come up. Share my rest and
splendour till all natures that were your enemies become slaves to
dance before you and backs for you to ride, and firmness for your
feet to rest on.

From beyond all place and time, out of the very Place, authority
will be given you: the strengths that once opposed your will shall
be obedient fire in your blood and heavenly thunder in your voice.

Overcome us that, so overcome, we may be ourselves: we desire
the beginning of your reign as we desire dawn and dew, wetness
at the birth of light.

Master, your Master has appointed you for ever: to be our King
of Justice and our high Priest.

Boy into Dragon

MEANWHILE Eustace slept and slept—and slept. What woke
him was a pain in his arm. The moon was shining in at the
mouth of the cave, and the bed of treasures seemed to have
grown much more comfortable: in fact he could hardly feel
it at all. He was puzzled by the pain in his arm at first, but
presently it occurred to him that the bracelet which he had
shoved up above his elbow had become strangely tight. His

arm must have swollen while he was asleep (it was his left arm).

He moved his right arm in order to feel his left, but stopped before he had moved it an inch and bit his lip in terror. For just in front of him, and a little on his right, where the moonlight fell clear on the floor of the cave, he saw a hideous shape moving. He knew that shape: it was a dragon's claw. It had moved as he moved his hand and became still when he stopped moving his hand.

"Oh, what a fool I've been," thought Eustace. "Of course, the brute had a mate and it's lying beside me."

For several minutes he did not dare to move a muscle. He saw two thin columns of smoke going up before his eyes, black against the moonlight; just as there had been smoke coming from the dragon's nose before it died. This was so alarming that he held his breath. The two columns of smoke vanished. When he could hold his breath no longer he let it out stealthily; instantly two jets of smoke appeared again. But even yet he had no idea of the truth.

Presently he decided that he would edge very cautiously to his left and try to creep out of the cave. Perhaps the creature was asleep—and anyway it was his only chance. But of course before he edged to the left he looked to the left. Oh horror! there was a dragon's claw on that side, too.

No one will blame Eustace if at this moment he shed tears. He was surprised at the size of his own tears as he saw them splashing on to the treasure in front of him. They also seemed strangely hot; steam went up from them.

But there was no good crying. He must try to crawl out from between the two dragons. He began extending his right arm. The dragon's foreleg and claw on his right went through exactly the same motion. Then he thought he would try his left. The dragon limb on that side moved, too.

Two dragons, one on each side, mimicking whatever he did! His nerve broke and he simply made a bolt for it.

There was such a clatter and rasping, and clinking of

gold, and grinding of stones, as he rushed out of the cave that he thought they were both following him. He daren't look back. He rushed to the pool. The twisted shape of the dead dragon lying in the moonlight would have been enough to frighten anyone but now he hardly noticed it. His idea was to get into the water.

But just as he reached the edge of the pool two things happened. First of all it came over him like a thunderclap that he had been running on all fours—and why on earth had he been doing that? And secondly, as he bent towards the water, he thought for a second that yet another dragon was staring up at him out of the pool. But in an instant he realised the truth. That dragon face in the pool was his own reflection. There was no doubt of it. It moved as he moved: it opened and shut its mouth as he opened and shut his.

He had turned into a dragon while he was asleep. Sleeping on a dragon's hoard with greedy, dragonish thoughts in his heart, he had become a dragon himself.

That explained everything. There had been no two dragons beside him in the cave. The claws to right and left had been his own right and left claws. The two columns of smoke had been coming from his own nostrils. As for the pain in his left arm (or what had been his left arm) he could now see what had happened by squinting with his left eye. The bracelet which had fitted very nicely on the upper arm of a boy was far too small for the thick, stumpy foreleg of a dragon. It had sunk deeply into his scaly flesh and there was a throbbing bulge on each side of it. He tore at the place with his dragon's teeth but could not get it off.

Dragon Back into Boy

"WELL, ANYWAY, I LOOKED UP and saw the very last thing I expected: a huge lion coming slowly towards me. And one queer thing was that there was no moon last night, but there was moonlight where the lion was. So it came nearer and nearer. I was terribly afraid of it. You may think that, being a dragon, I could have knocked any lion out easily enough. But it wasn't that kind of fear. I wasn't afraid of it eating me, I was just afraid of *it*—if you can understand. Well, it came closer up to me and looked straight into my eyes. And I shut my eyes tight. But that wasn't any good because it told me to follow it."

"You mean it spoke?"

"I don't know. Now that you mention it, I don't think it did. But it told me all the same. And I knew I'd have to do what it told me, so I got up and followed it. And it led me a long way into the mountains. And there was always this moonlight over and round the lion wherever we went. So at last we came to the top of a mountain I'd never seen before and on the top of this mountain there was a garden—trees and fruit and everything. In the middle of it there was a well.

"I knew it was a well because you could see the water bubbling up from the bottom of it: but it was a lot bigger than most wells—like a very big, round bath with marble steps going down into it. The water was as clear as anything and I thought if I could get in there and bathe it would ease the pain in my leg. But the lion told me I must undress first. Mind you, I don't know if he said any words out loud or not.

"I was just going to say that I couldn't undress because I hadn't any clothes on when I suddenly thought that dragons are snaky sort of things and snakes can cast their skins. Oh, of course, thought I, that's what the lion means. So I started scratching myself and my scales began coming off all over the place. And then I scratched a little deeper and, instead of just scales coming off here and there, my whole skin started peeling off beautifully, like it does after an illness, or as if I was a banana. In a minute or two I just stepped out of it. I could see it lying there beside me, looking rather nasty. It was a most lovely feeling. So I started to go down into the well for my bathe.

"But just as I was going to put my foot into the water I looked down and saw that it was all hard and rough and wrinkled and scaly just as it had been before. Oh, that's all right, said I, it only means I had another smaller suit on underneath the first one, and I'll have to get out of it too. So I scratched and tore again and this under skin peeled off beautifully and out I stepped and left it lying beside the other one and went down to the well for my bathe.

"Well, exactly the same thing happened again. And I thought to myself, oh dear, how ever many skins have I got to take off? For I was longing to bathe my leg. So I scratched away for the third time and got off a third skin, just like the two others, and stepped out of it. But as soon as I looked at myself in the water I knew it had been no good.

"Then the lion said—but I don't know if it spoke—You will have to let me undress you. I was afraid of his claws, I can tell you, but I was pretty nearly desperate now. So I just lay flat down on my back to let him do it.

"The very first tear he made was so deep that I thought it had gone right into my heart. And when he began pulling the skin off, it hurt worse than anything I've ever felt. The only thing that made me able to bear it was just the pleasure of feeling the stuff peel off. You know—if you've ever picked the scab of a sore place. It hurts like billy-oh but it *is* such fun to see it coming away."

"I know exactly what you mean," said Edmund.

"Well, he peeled the beastly stuff right off—just as I thought I'd done it myself the other three times, only they hadn't hurt—and there it was lying on the grass: only ever so much thicker, and darker, and more knobbly looking than the others had been. And there was I as smooth and soft as a peeled switch and smaller than I had been. Then he caught hold of me—I didn't like that much for I was very tender underneath now that I'd no skin on—and threw me into the water. It smarted like anything but only for a moment. After that it became perfectly delicious and as soon as I started swimming and splashing I found that all the pain had gone from my arm. And then I saw why. I'd turned into a boy again. You'd think me simply phoney if I told you how I felt about my own arms. I know they've no muscle and are pretty mouldy compared with Caspian's, but I was so glad to see them.

"After a bit the lion took me out and dressed me—"

"Dressed you. With his paws?"

"Well, I don't exactly remember that bit. But he did somehow or other: in new clothes—the same I've got on now, as a matter of fact. And then suddenly I was back here. Which is what makes me think it must have been a dream."

"No. It wasn't a dream," said Edmund.

"Why not?"

"Well, there are the clothes, for one thing. And you have been—well, un-dragoned, for another."

"What do you think it was, then?" asked Eustace.

"I think you've seen Aslan," said Edmund.

"Aslan!" said Eustace. "I've heard that name mentioned several times since we joined the *Dawn Treader*. And I felt—I don't know what—I hated it. But, I was hating everything then. And by the way, I'd like to apologise. I'm afraid I've been pretty beastly."

The Seven Deadly Sins

DEADLY SINS

Through our lives thy meshes run
Deft as spiders' catenation,
Crossed and crossed again and spun
Finer than the fiend's temptation.

Greed into herself would turn
All that's sweet: but let her follow
Still that path, and greed will learn
How the whole world is hers to swallow.

Sloth that would find out a bed
Blind to morning, deaf to waking,
Shuffling shall at last be led
To the peace that knows no breaking.

Lechery, that feels sharp lust
Sharper from each promised staying,
Goes at long last—go she must—
Where alone is sure allaying.

Anger, postulating still
Inexcusables to shatter,
From the shelter of thy will
Finds herself her proper matter.

Envy had rather die than see
Other's course her own outflying;
She will pay with death to be
Where her Best brooks no denying.

Pride, that from each step, anew
Mounts again with mad aspiring,
Must find all at last, save you,
Set too low for her desiring.

Avarice, while she finds an end,
Counts but small the largest treasure.
Whimperingly at last she'll bend
To take free what has no measure.

So inexorably thou
On thy shattered foes pursuing,
Never a respite dost allow
Save what works their own undoing.

Take Your Choice

He [GEORGE MACDONALD] was silent for a few minutes, and
then began again.

"Ye'll understand, there are innumerable forms of this
choice. Sometimes forms that one hardly thought of at all
on earth. There was a creature came here not long ago and
went back—Sir Archibald they called him. In his earthly life
he'd been interested in nothing but Survival. He'd written
a whole shelf-full of books about it. He began by being
philosophical, but in the end he took up Psychical Research. It grew to be his only occupation—experimenting,
lecturing, running a magazine. And travelling too: digging
out queer stories among Thibetan lamas and being initiated
into brotherhoods in Central Africa. Proofs—and more
proofs—and then more proofs again—were what he
wanted. It drove him mad if ever he saw anyone taking an

interest in anything else. He got into trouble during one of
your wars for running up and down the country telling
them not to fight because it wasted a lot of money that
ought to be spent on Research. Well, in good time, the poor
creature died and came here: and there was no power in the
universe would have prevented him staying and going on
to the mountains. But do ye think that did him any good?
This country was no use to him at all. Everyone here had
'survived' already. Nobody took the least interest in the
question. There was nothing more to prove. His occupation
was clean gone. Of course if he would only have admitted
that he'd mistaken the means for the end and had a good
laugh at himself he could have begun all over again like a
little child and entered into joy. But he would not do that.
He cared nothing about joy. In the end he went away."

"How fantastic!" said I.

"Do ye think so?" said the Teacher with a piercing
glance. "It is nearer to such as you than ye think. There
have been men before now who got so interested in prov-
ing the existence of God that they came to care nothing for
God Himself . . . as if the good Lord had nothing to do but
exist! There have been some who were so occupied in
spreading Christianity that they never gave a thought to
Christ. Man! Ye see it in smaller matters. Did ye never
know a lover of books that with all his first editions and
signed copies had lost the power to read them? Or an or-
ganiser of charities that had lost all love for the poor? It is
the subtlest of all the snares."

Moved by a desire to change the subject, I asked why the
Solid People, since they were full of love, did not go down
into Hell to rescue the Ghosts. Why were they content simply to meet them on the plain? One would have expected a
more militant charity.

"Ye will understand that better, perhaps, before ye go,"
said he. "In the meantime, I must tell ye they have come
further for the sake of the Ghosts than ye can understand.

Every one of us lives only to journey further and further into the mountains. Every one of us has interrupted that journey and retraced immeasurable distances to come down today on the mere chance of saving some Ghosts. Of course it is also joy to do so, but ye cannot blame us for that! And it would be no use to come further even if it were possible. The sane would do no good if they made themselves mad to help madmen."

"But what of the poor Ghosts who never get into the omnibus at all?"

"Everyone who wishes it does. Never fear. There are only two kinds of people in the end: those who say to God, 'Thy will be done,' and those to whom God says, in the end, *'Thy* will be done.' All that are in Hell, choose it. Without that self-choice there could be no Hell. No soul that seriously and constantly desires joy will ever miss it. Those who seek find. To those who knock it is opened."

Willful Disbelief

BUT THE RESULT WHICH FOLLOWED was simply wretched. There was a feeble attempt from a few Dwarfs (about five) which died away all at once: from several others there were sulky growls. Many said nothing at all.

"Don't they understand?" said Jill impatiently.

"What's wrong with all you Dwarfs? Don't you hear what the King says? It's all over. The Ape isn't going to rule Narnia any longer. Everyone can go back to ordinary life. You can have fun again. Aren't you glad?"

After a pause of nearly a minute a not-very-nice looking Dwarf with hair and beard as black as soot said:

"And who might you be, Missie?"

"I'm Jill," she said. "The same Jill who rescued King

Rilian from the enchantment—and this is Eustace who did it too—and we've come back from another world after hundreds of years. Aslan sent us."

The Dwarfs all looked at one another with grins; sneering grins, not merry ones.

"Well," said the Black Dwarf (whose name was Griffle), "I don't know how all you chaps feel, but I feel I've heard as much about Aslan as I want to for the rest of my life."

"That's right, that's right," growled the other Dwarfs. "It's all a trick, all a blooming trick."

"What do you mean?" said Tirian. He had not been pale when he was fighting but he was pale now. He had thought this was going to be a beautiful moment, but it was turning out more like a bad dream.

"You must think we're blooming soft in the head, that you must," said Griffle. "We've been taken in once and now you expect us to be taken in again the next minute. We've no more use for stories about Aslan, see! Look at him! An old moke with long ears!"

"By heaven, you make me mad," said Tirian. "Which of us said *that* was Aslan? That is the Ape's imitation of the real Aslan. Can't you understand?"

"And you've got a better imitation, I suppose!" said Griffle. "No thanks. We've been fooled once and we're not going to be fooled again."

"I have not," said Tirian angrily, "I serve the real Aslan."

"Where's he? Who's he? Show him to us!" said several Dwarfs.

"Do you think I keep him in my wallet, fools?" said Tirian. "Who am I that I could make Aslan appear at my bidding? He's not a tame lion."

The moment those words were out of his mouth he realised that he had made a false move. The Dwarfs at once began repeating "not a tame lion, not a tame lion," in a jeering singsong. "That's what the other lot kept on telling us," said one.

"Do you mean you don't believe in the real Aslan?" said Jill. "But I've seen him. And he has sent us two here out of a different world."

"Ah," said Griffle with a broad smile. "So *you* say. They've taught you your stuff all right. Saying your lessons, ain't you?"

"Churl," cried Tirian, "will you give a lady a lie to her very face?"

"You keep a civil tongue in your head, Mister," replied the Dwarf. "I don't think we want any more kings—if you *are* Tirian, which you don't look like him—no more than we want any Aslans. We're going to look after ourselves from now on and touch our caps to nobody. See?"

"That's right," said the other Dwarfs. "We're on our own now. No more Aslan, no more kings, no more silly stories about other worlds. The Dwarfs are for the Dwarfs." And they began to fall into their places and to get ready for marching back to wherever they had come from.

"Little beasts!" said Eustace. "Aren't you even going to say *thank you* for being saved from the salt-mines?"

"Oh, we know all about that," said Griffle, over his shoulder. "You wanted to make use of us, that's why you rescued us. You're playing some game of your own. Come on you chaps."

And the Dwarfs struck up the queer little marching song which goes with the drumbeat, and off they tramped into the darkness.

Weston Gets Religion

"The utility of the human race," continued Weston, "in the long run depends rigidly on the possibility of inter-planetary, and even inter-sidereal, travel. That problem I solved. The key of human destiny was placed in my hands.

It would be unnecessary—and painful to us both—to remind you how it was wrenched from me in Malacandra by
a member of a hostile intelligent species whose existence, I
admit, I had not anticipated."

"Not hostile exactly," said Ransom, "but go on."

"The rigours of our return journey from Malacandra led
to a serious breakdown in my health——"

"Mine too," said Ransom.

Weston looked somewhat taken aback at the interruption
and went on. "During my convalescence I had that leisure
for reflection which I had denied myself for many years. In
particular I reflected on the objections you had felt to that
liquidation of the non-human inhabitants of Malacandra
which was, of course, the necessary preliminary to its occupation by our own species. The traditional and, if I may
say so, the humanitarian form in which you advanced those
objections had till then concealed from me their true
strength. That strength I now began to perceive. I began to
see that my own exclusive devotion to human utility was
really based on an unconscious dualism."

"What do you mean?"

"I mean that all my life I had been making a wholly un-
scientific dichotomy or antithesis between Man and Nature—had conceived myself fighting *for* Man against his
non-human environment. During my illness I plunged into
Biology, and particularly into what may be called biological
philosophy. Hitherto, as a physicist, I had been content to
regard Life as a subject outside my scope. The conflicting
views of those who drew a sharp line between the organic
and the inorganic and those who held that what we call Life
was inherent in matter from the very beginning had not
interested me. Now it did. I saw almost at once that I could
admit no break, no discontinuity, in the unfolding of the
cosmic process. I became a convinced believer in emergent
evolution. All is one. The stuff of mind, the unconsciously
purposive dynamism, is present from the very beginning."

Here he paused. Ransom had heard this sort of thing pretty often before and wondered when his companion was coming to the point. When Weston resumed it was with an even deeper solemnity of tone.

"The majestic spectacle of this blind, inarticulate purposiveness thrusting its way upward and ever upward in an endless unity of differentiated achievements towards an ever-increasing complexity of organisation, towards spontaneity and spirituality, swept away all my old conception of a duty to Man as such. Man in himself is nothing. The forward movement of Life—the growing spirituality—is everything. I say to you quite freely, Ransom, that I should have been wrong in liquidating the Malacandrians. It was a mere prejudice that made me prefer our own race to theirs. To spread spirituality, not to spread the human race, is henceforth my mission. This sets the coping-stone on my career. I worked first for myself; then for science; then for humanity; but now at last for Spirit itself—I might say, borrowing language which will be more familiar to you, the Holy Spirit."

"Now what exactly do you mean by that?" asked Ransom.

"I mean," said Weston, "that nothing now divides you and me except a few outworn theological technicalities with which organised religion has unhappily allowed itself to get incrusted. But I have penetrated that crust. The Meaning beneath it is as true and living as ever. If you will excuse me for putting it that way, the essential truth of the religious view of life finds a remarkable witness in the fact that it enabled you, on Malacandra, to grasp in your own mythical and imaginative fashion, a truth which was hidden from me."

Religious Instruction

THEN A YEAR WENT PAST, and one dark, cold, wet morning John was made to put on new clothes. They were the ugliest clothes that had ever been put upon him, which John did not mind at all, but they also caught him under the chin, and were tight under the arms, which he minded a great deal, and they made him itch all over. And his father and mother took him out along the road, one holding him by each hand (which was uncomfortable, too, and very unnecessary), and told him they were taking him to see the Steward. The Steward lived in a big dark house of stone on the side of the road. The father and mother went in to talk to the Steward first, and John was left sitting in the hall on a chair so high that his feet did not reach the floor. There were other chairs in the hall where he could have sat in comfort, but his father had told him that the Steward would be very angry if he did not sit absolutely still and be very good: and John was beginning to be afraid, so he sat still in the high chair with his feet dangling, and his clothes itching all over him, and his eyes starting out of his head. After a very long time his parents came back again, looking as if they had been with the doctor, very grave. Then they said that John must go in and see the Steward too. And when John came into the room, there was an old man with a red, round face, who was very kind and full of jokes, so that John quite got over his fears, and they had a good talk about fishing tackle and bicycles. But just when the talk was at its best, the Steward got up and cleared his throat. He then took down a mask from the wall with a long white beard attached to it and suddenly clapped it on his face, so that his appearance was awful. And he said, "Now I am going to talk to you about the Landlord. The Landlord owns all the country, and it is *very, very* kind of him to allow us to live on it at all—very, very kind." He went on repeating "very kind" in a queer singsong voice so long that John would have laughed, but that now he was beginning to be frightened again. The Steward then took down from a peg a big card with small print all over it, and said, "Here is a list of all the things the Landlord says you must not do. You'd better look at it." So John took the card: but half the rules seemed to forbid things he had never heard of, and the other half forbade things he was doing every day and could not imagine not doing: and the number of the rules was so enormous that he felt he could never remember them all. "I hope," said the Steward, "that you have not already broken any of the rules?" John's heart began to thump, and his eyes bulged more and more, and he was at his wit's end when the Steward took the mask off and looked at John with his real face and said, "Better tell a lie, old chap, better tell a lie. Easiest for all concerned," and popped the mask on his face all in a flash. John gulped and said quickly, "Oh, no, sir." "That is just as well," said the Steward through the mask. "Because, you know, if you did break any of them and the Landlord got to know of it, do you know what he'd do to you?" "No, sir," said John: and the Steward's eyes seemed to be twinkling dreadfully through the holes of the mask. "He'd take you and shut you up for ever and ever in a black hole full of snakes and scorpions as large as lobsters—for ever and ever. And besides that, he is such a kind, good man, so very, very kind, that I am sure you would never *want* to displease him." "No, sir," said John. "But, please, sir . . ." "Well," said the Steward. "Please, sir, supposing I did break one, one little one, just by accident, you know. Could nothing stop the snakes and lobsters?" "Ah! . . ." said the Steward; and then he sat down and talked for a long time, but John could not understand a single syllable. However, it all ended with pointing out that the Landlord was quite extraordinarily kind and good to his tenants, and would certainly torture most of them to death the moment he had the slightest pretext. "And you can't blame him," said the Steward. "For after all, it *is* his land, and it is so very good of him to let us live here at all—people like us, you know." Then the Steward took off the mask and had a nice, sensible chat with John again, and gave him a cake and brought him out to his father and mother. But just as they were going he bent down and whispered in John's ear, "I shouldn't bother about it all too much if I were you." At the same time he slipped the card of the rules into John's hand and told him he could keep it for his own use.

Diluted Religion

"THANK YOU," said John, "but if you can give me some directions I think I would like to continue my journey, I am trying to find an Island in the West—"

"That is a beautiful idea," said Mr. Broad. "And if you will trust an older traveller, the seeking is the finding. How many happy days you have before you!"

"And I want to know," continued John, "whether it is really necessary to cross the canyon."

"To be sure you do. I wouldn't 'for the world hold you back. At the same time, my dear boy, I think there is a very real danger at your age of trying to make these things too definite. That has been the great error of my profession in past ages. We have tried to enclose everything in formulae, to turn poetry into logic, and metaphor into dogma; and now that we are beginning to realize our mistake we find ourselves shackled by the formulae of dead men. I don't say that they were not adequate once: but they have ceased to be adequate for us with our wider knowledge. When I became a man, I put away childish things. These great truths need re-interpretation in every age."

"I am not sure that I quite understand," said John. "Do you mean that I must cross the canyon or that I must not?"

"I see you want to pin me down," said Mr. Broad, with a smile, "and I love to see it. I was like that myself once. But one loses faith in abstract logic as one grows older. Do you never feel that the truth is so great and so simple that no mere words can contain it? The heaven and the heaven of heavens . . . how much less this house that I have builded."

"Well, anyway," said John, deciding to try a new question. "Supposing a man *did* have to cross the canyon. Is it true that he would have to rely on Mother Kirk?"

"Ah, Mother Kirk! I love and honour her from the bottom of my heart, but I trust that loving her does not mean being blind to her faults. We are none of us infallible. If I sometimes feel that I must differ from her at present, it is because I honour all the more the *idea* that she stands for, the thing she may yet become. For the moment, there is no denying that she has let herself get a little out of date. Surely, for many of our generation, there is a truer, a more acceptable, message in all this beautiful world around us? I don't know whether you are anything of a botanist. If you would care—"

"I want my Island," said John. "Can you tell me how to reach it? I am afraid I am not specially interested in botany."

"It would open a new world to you," said Mr. Broad. "A new window on the Infinite. But perhaps this is not in your line. We must all find our own key to the mystery after all. I wouldn't for the world . . ."

"I think I must be going," said John. "And I have enjoyed myself very much. If I follow this road, shall I find anywhere that will give me a night's lodging in a few miles?"

The Apostate Bishop

"No," said the other. "I can promise you none of these things. No sphere of usefulness: you are not needed there at all. No scope for your talents: only forgiveness for having perverted them. No atmosphere of inquiry, for I will bring you to the land not of questions but of answers, and you shall see the face of God."

"Ah, but we must all interpret those beautiful words in our own way! For me there is no such thing as a final answer. The free wind of inquiry must *always* continue to blow through the mind, must it not? 'Prove all things' . . . to travel hopefully is better than to arrive."

"If that were true, and known to be true, how could anyone travel hopefully? There would be nothing to hope for."

"But you must feel yourself that there is something stifling about the idea of finality? Stagnation, my dear boy, what is more soul-destroying than stagnation?"

"You think that, because hitherto you have experienced truth only with the abstract intellect. I will bring you where you can taste it like honey and be embraced by it as by a bridegroom. Your thirst shall be quenched."

"Well, really, you know, I am not aware of a thirst for some ready-made truth which puts an end to intellectual activity in the way you seem to be describing. Will it leave me the free play of Mind, Dick? I must insist on that, you know."

"Free, as a man is free to drink while he is drinking. He

is not free still to be dry." The Ghost seemed to think for a moment. "I can make nothing of that idea," it said.

"Listen!" said the White Spirit. "Once you were a child. Once you knew what inquiry was for. There was a time when you asked questions because you wanted answers, and were glad when you had found them. Become that child again: even now."

"Ah, but when I became a man I put away childish things."

"You have gone far wrong. Thirst was made for water; inquiry for truth. What you now call the free play of inquiry has neither more nor less to do with the ends for which intelligence was given you than masturbation has to do with marriage."

"If we cannot be reverent, there is at least no need to be obscene. The suggestion that I should return at any age to the mere factual inquisitiveness of boyhood strikes me as preposterous. In any case, that question-and-answer conception of thought only applies to matters of fact. Religious and speculative questions are surely on a different level."

"We know nothing of religion here: we think only of Christ. We know nothing of speculation. Come and see. I will bring you to Eternal Fact, the Father of all other fact-hood."

"I should object very strongly to describing God as a 'fact.' The Supreme Value would surely be a less inadequate description. It is hardly . . ."

"Do you not even believe that He exists?"

"Exists? What does Existence mean? You *will* keep on implying some sort of static, ready-made reality which is, so to speak, 'there,' and to which our minds have simply to conform. These great mysteries cannot be approached in that way. If there were such a thing (there is no need to interrupt, my dear boy) quite frankly, I should not be interested in it. It would be of no *religious* significance. God, for me, is something purely spiritual. The spirit of sweetness and light and tolerance—and, er, service, Dick, service. We mustn't forget that, you know."

"If the thirst of the Reason is really dead . . . ," said the Spirit, and then stopped as though pondering. Then suddenly he said, "Can you, at least, still desire happiness?"

"Happiness, my dear Dick," said the Ghost placidly, "happiness, as you will come to see when you are older, lies in the path of duty. Which reminds me. . . . Bless my soul, I'd nearly forgotten. Of course I can't come with you. I have to be back next Friday to read a paper. We have a little Theological Society down there. Oh yes! there is plenty of intellectual life. Not of a very high quality, perhaps. One notices a certain lack of grip—a certain confusion of mind. That is where I can be of some use to them. There are even regrettable jealousies. . . . I don't know why, but tempers seem less controlled than they used to be. Still, one mustn't expect too much of human nature. I feel I can do a great work among them. But you've never asked me what my paper is about! I'm taking the text about growing up to the measure of the stature of Christ and working out an idea which I feel sure you'll be interested in. I'm going to point out how people always forget that Jesus (here the Ghost bowed) was a comparatively young man when he died. He would have outgrown some of his earlier views, you know, if he'd lived. As he might have done, with a little more tact and patience. I am going to ask my audience to consider what his mature views would have been. A profoundly interesting question. What a different Christianity we might have had if only the Founder had reached his full stature! I shall end up by pointing out how this deepens the significance of the Crucifixion. One feels for the first time what a disaster it was: what a tragic waste . . . so much promise cut short. Oh, must you be going? Well, so must I. Goodbye, my dear boy. It has been a great pleasure. Most stimulating and provocative. Goodbye, goodbye, goodbye."

The Ghost nodded its head and beamed on the Spirit with a bright clerical smile—or with the best approach to it which such unsubstantial lips could manage—and then turned away humming softly to itself "City of God, how broad and far."

*Church and State**

The Leader takes a turn and rubs his
  hands,
Chuckling and murmuring "Who'd
  have thought it now?"
And then he comes where the Arch-
  bishop stands
And pulls the old man to him by the
  sleeve
Into a window, with a graver brow
Politically furrowed. "I believe
We know each other pretty well," said
  he,
"Experienced people seldom disagree.
You see there's been a change. I'm
  called to fill
The supreme office, by the people's will
Or, strictly, what the people will dis-
  cover
To have been their will when all the
  shouting's over.
Now, in this new regime, of course
  your Grace
Must certainly retain his present place
And power and temporalities. Indeed,
If I might criticise, we rather need
Not less but more of what you repre-
  sent;
For up till now—pray, take this as it's
  meant,

---

*From *The Queen of Drum*.

Kindly—a certain somnolence has come
To be the hall mark of the Church of
    Drum,
For several years. Henceforward that
    won't do;
And naturally I rely on you.
Faith—martyrdom—and all that side of
    things
Concerns Dictators even more than
    Kings.
Can you contrive a really hot revival,
A state religion that allows no rival?
You understand, henceforth it's got to
    be
A Drummian kind of Christianity—
A good old Drummian god who has al-
    ways some
Peculiar purpose up His sleeve for
    Drum,
Something that makes the increase of
    our trade
And territories feel like a Crusade,
Or, even if neither should in fact in-
    crease,
Teaches men in my will to find their
    peace.
Those are the general principles. But
    now
The problem is (and you must show me
    how)
To deal with the late sovereign's disap-
    pearance.
I doubt if they'd believe in interference
From Heaven direct—a plain, Old Tes-
    tament
Annihilation on the tyrant sent . . .

But, short of that, we either must produce
The corpse, or else some plausible excuse.
What do you think? The matter's in
your line
And suited to your office more than
mine."

The Bishop answered, "Any man in the
world
Has more right to rebuke these words
than I.
But I believe—I know you could not
know
That I believed—in God. I dare not lie."

The General answered, "I should hope
you do;
I'm a religious man as well as you,
But now we're talking politics. You say
That you believe; the point is, so do
they,
Which makes all doctrines easy to di-
gest.
Come, now; I've made a very small re-
quest."

"I cannot tell them more than I believe.
I dare not play with such immeasur-
ables.
I am afraid: yes, that's the truth, afraid,
Put it no higher. Fear would stop my
tongue."

The Leader said, "Oh Lord, to have a
fool

To deal with. God Almighty, keep me
   cool!
What do you fear? Have I not made it
   plain,
You and your Church have everything
   to gain?
Be loyal to the Leader and I'll build
Cathedrals for you, yes, and see them
   filled,
I'll give you a free hand to bait all Jews
And infidels. You can't mean to
   refuse?"

"I must: for He of whom I am afraid
Esteems the gifts that you can promise
   me
Evil, or else of very small account."

"Silence!" The Leader said, "Silence, I
   say!
You never talked like this before to-day,
And now to make religion your pret-
   ence,
Frankly, I hold it sheer irreverence.
If you look down from such a starry
   height
As that, upon all earthly power and
   might,
Why, in God's name, have you not told
   us so
A year, or ten, or fifteen years ago?
Why was your other-worldliness so
   dumb
When every office went for sale in
   Drum,

When half the people had no bread to
   eat
Because the Chancellor'd cornered all
   the wheat,
When the Queen played her witchery
   nights, and when
The old King had his women nine or
   ten?
All this you saw, unless you were
   asleep.
God! to sit still beside the course and
   keep
Your malice hid, till at the race's end
You dart your leg out to trip up a friend
Just at the goal. I'd counted upon you—
The thing so dangerous and my friends
   so few,
Would I have risked it if I thought the
   Church
Was going to turn and leave me in the
   lurch?
What? Silent still? Why then, damna-
   tion take you!
I've begged enough, I'll find a way to
   make you.
You've played a dirty trick, and now
   you'll rue it!"
He called his men and said, "Boys! Put
   him through it."

Religious Syncretism

"PLEASE," said the Lamb, "I can't understand. What have we to do with the Calormenes? We belong to Aslan. They belong to Tash. They have a god called Tash. They say he has four arms and the head of a vulture. They kill Men on his altar. I don't believe there's any such person as Tash. But if there was, how could Aslan be friends with him?"

All the animals cocked their heads sideways and all their bright eyes flashed towards the Ape. They knew it was the best question anyone had asked yet.

The Ape jumped up and spat at the Lamb.

"Baby!" he hissed. "Silly little bleater! Go home to your mother and drink milk. What do you understand of such things? But you others, listen. Tash is only another name for Aslan. All that old idea of us being right and the Calormenes wrong is silly. We know better now. The Calormenes use different words but we all mean the same thing. Tash and Aslan are only two different names for you know Who. That's why there can never be any quarrel between them. Get that into your heads, you stupid brutes. Tash is Aslan: Aslan is Tash."

You know how sad your own dog's face can look sometimes. Think of that and then think of all the faces of those Talking Beasts—all those honest, humble, bewildered birds, bears, badgers, rabbits, moles, and mice—all far sadder than that. Every tail was down, every whisker drooped. It would have broken your heart with very pity to see their faces. There was only one who did not look at all unhappy.

It was a ginger cat—a great big Tom in the prime of life— who sat bolt upright with his tail curled round his toes, in the very front row of all the Beasts. He had been staring hard at the Ape and the Calormene captain all the time and had never once blinked his eyes.

"Excuse me," said the Cat very politely, "but this interests me. Does your friend from Calormen say the same?"

"Assuredly," said the Calormene. "The enlightened Ape—Man, I mean—is in the right. *Aslan* means neither less nor more than *Tash.*"

"Especially, Aslan means *no more* than Tash?" suggested the Cat.

"No more at all," said the Calormene, looking the Cat straight in the face.

"Is that good enough for you, Ginger?" said the Ape.

"Oh certainly," said Ginger coolly. "Thank you very much. I only wanted to be quite clear. I think I am beginning to understand."

Up till now the King and Jewel had said nothing: they were waiting until the Ape should bid them speak, for they thought it was no use interrupting. But now, as Tirian looked round on the miserable faces of the Narnians, and saw how they would all believe that Aslan and Tash were one and the same, he could bear it no longer.

"Ape," he cried with a great voice, "you lie. You lie damnably. You lie like like a Calormene. You lie like an Ape."

He meant to go on and ask how the terrible god Tash who fed on the blood of his people could possibly be the same as the good Lion by whose blood all Narnia was saved. If he had been allowed to speak, the rule of the Ape might have ended that day; the Beasts might have seen the truth and thrown the Ape down. But before he could say another word two Calormenes struck him in the mouth with all their force, and a third, from behind, kicked his feet from under him. And as he fell, the Ape squealed in rage and terror:

"Take him away. Take him away. Take him where he

cannot hear us, nor we hear him. There tie him to a tree. I will—I mean, Aslan will—do justice to him later.''

The Reluctant Antichrist

AS SOON AS HE WAS ALONE Shift went shambling along, sometimes on two paws and sometimes on four, till he reached his own tree. Then he swung himself up from branch to branch, chattering and grinning all the time, and went into his little house. He found needle and thread and a big pair of scissors there; for he was a clever Ape and the Dwarfs had taught him how to sew. He put the ball of thread (it was very thick stuff, more like cord than thread) into his mouth so that his cheek bulged out as if he were sucking a big bit of toffee. He held the needle between his lips and took the scissors in his left paw. Then he came down the tree and shambled across to the lionskin. He squatted down and got to work.

He saw at once that the body of the lionskin would be too long for Puzzle and its neck too short. So he cut a good piece out of the body and used it to make a long collar for Puzzle's long neck. Then he cut off the head and sewed the collar in between the head and the shoulders. He put threads on both sides of the skin so that it would tie up under Puzzle's chest and stomach. Every now and then a bird would pass overhead and Shift would stop his work, looking up anxiously. He did not want anyone to see what he was doing. But none of the birds he saw were Talking Birds, so it didn't matter.

Late in the afternoon Puzzle came back. He was not trotting but only plodding patiently along, the way donkeys do.

"There weren't any oranges," he said, "and there weren't any bananas. And I'm very tired." He lay down.

"Come and try on your beautiful new lionskin coat," said Shift.

"Oh bother that old skin," said Puzzle, "I'll try it on in the morning. I'm too tired tonight."

"You *are* unkind, Puzzle," said Shift. "If *you're* tired, what do you think *I* am? All day long, while you've been having a lovely refreshing walk down the valley, I've been working hard to make you a coat. My paws are so tired I can hardly hold these scissors. And now you won't say thank-you—and you won't even look at the coat—and you don't care—and—and—"

"My dear Shift," said Puzzle getting up at once, "I am so sorry. I've been horrid. Of course I'd love to try it on. And it looks simply splendid. Do try it on me at once. Please do."

"Well, stand still then," said the Ape. The skin was very heavy for him to lift, but in the end, with a lot of pulling and pushing and puffing and blowing, he got it onto the donkey. He tied it underneath Puzzle's body and he tied the legs to Puzzle's legs and the tail to Puzzle's tail. A good deal of Puzzle's grey nose and face could be seen through the open mouth of the lion's head. No one who had ever seen a real lion would have been taken in for a moment. But if someone who had never seen a lion looked at Puzzle in his lionskin, he just might mistake him for a lion, if he didn't come too close, and if the light was not too good, and if Puzzle didn't let out a bray and didn't make any noise with his hoofs.

"You look wonderful, wonderful," said the Ape. "If anyone saw you now, they'd think you were Aslan, the Great Lion, himself."

"That would be dreadful," said Puzzle.

"No it wouldn't," said Shift. "Everyone would do whatever you told them."

"But I don't want to tell them anything."

"But think of the good we could do!" said Shift. "You'd have me to advise you, you know. I'd think of sensible orders for you to give. And everyone would have to obey us, even the King himself. We would set everything right in Narnia."

"But isn't everything right already?" said Puzzle.

"What!" cried Shift. "Everything right?—when there are no oranges or bananas?"

"Well, you know," said Puzzle, "there aren't many people—in fact, I don't think there's anyone but yourself—who wants those sort of things."

"There's sugar too," said Shift.

"H'm, yes," said the Ass. "It would be nice if there was more sugar."

"Well then, that's settled," said the Ape. "You will pretend to be Aslan, and I'll tell you what to say."

"No, no, no," said Puzzle. "Don't say such dreadful things. It would be wrong, Shift. I may be not very clever but I know that much. What would become of us if the real Aslan turned up?"

"I expect he'd be very pleased," said Shift. "Probably he sent us the lionskin on purpose, so that we could set things to right. Anyway, he never *does* turn up, you know. Not now-a-days."

At that moment there came a great thunderclap right overhead and the ground trembled with a small earthquake. Both the animals lost their balance and were flung on their faces.

"There!" gasped Puzzle, as soon as he had breath to speak. "It's a sign, a warning. I knew we were doing something dreadfully wicked. Take this wretched skin off me at once."

"No, no," said the Ape (whose mind worked very quickly). "It's a sign the other way. I was just going to say that if the real Aslan, as you call him, meant us to go on with this, he would send us a thunderclap and an earth-tremor. It was just on the tip of my tongue, only the sign itself came before I could get the words out. You've *got* to do it now, Puzzle. And please don't let us have any more arguing. You know you don't understand these things. What could a donkey know about signs?"

Gratification and Restraint

AT LONG LAST he reached the wooded part. There was an undergrowth of feathery vegetation, about the height of gooseberry bushes, coloured like sea anemones. Above this were the taller growths—strange trees with tube-like trunks of grey and purple spreading rich canopies above his head, in which orange, silver, and blue were the predominant colours. Here, with the aid of the tree trunks, he could keep his feet more easily. The smells in the forest were beyond all that he had ever conceived. To say that they made him feel hungry and thirsty would be misleading; almost, they created a new kind of hunger and thirst, a longing that seemed to flow over from the body into the soul and which was a heaven to feel. Again and again he stood still, clinging to some branch to steady himself, and breathed it all in, as if breathing had become a kind of ritual. And at the same time the forest landscape furnished what would have been a dozen landscapes on earth—now level wood with trees as vertical as towers, now a deep bottom where it was surprising not to find a stream, now a wood growing on a hillside, and now again, a hilltop whence one looked down through slanted boles at the distant sea. Save for the inorganic sound of waves there was utter silence about him. The sense of his solitude became intense without becoming at all painful—only adding, as it were, a last touch of wildness to the unearthly pleasures that surrounded him. If he had any fear now, it was a faint apprehension that his reason might be in danger. There was something in Perelandra that might overload a human brain.

Now he had come to a part of the wood where great globes of yellow fruit hung from the trees—clustered as toy-balloons are clustered on the back of the balloon-man and about the same size. He picked one of them and turned it over and over. The rind was smooth and firm and seemed impossible to tear open. Then by accident one of his fingers punctured it and went through into coldness. After a moment's hesitation he put the little aperture to his lips. He had meant to extract the smallest, experimental sip, but the first taste put his caution all to flight. It was, of course, a taste, just as his thirst and hunger had been thirst and hunger. But then it was so different from every other taste that it seemed mere pedantry to call it a taste at all. It was like the discovery of a totally new *genus* of pleasures, something unheard of among men, out of all reckoning, beyond all covenant. For one draught of this on earth wars would be fought and nations betrayed. It could not be classified. He could never tell us, when he came back to the world of men, whether it was sharp or sweet, savoury or voluptuous, creamy or piercing. "Not like that" was all he could ever say to such inquiries. As he let the empty gourd fall from his hand and was about to pluck a second one, it came into his head that he was now neither hungry nor thirsty. And yet to repeat a pleasure so intense and almost so spiritual seemed an obvious thing to do. His reason, or what we commonly take to be reason in our own world, was all in favour of tasting this miracle again; the childlike innocence of fruit, the labours he had undergone, the uncertainty of the future, all seemed to commend the action. Yet something seemed opposed to this "reason." It is difficult to suppose that this opposition came from desire, for what desire would turn from so much deliciousness? But for whatever cause, it appeared to him better not to taste again. Perhaps the experience had been so complete that repetition would be a vulgarity—like asking to hear the same symphony twice in a day.

War

FRENCH NOCTURNE

(MONCHY-LE-PREUX)

Long leagues on either hand the trenches spread
And all is still; now even this gross line
Drinks in the frosty silences divine,
The pale, green moon is riding overhead.

The jaws of a sacked village, stark and grim,
Out on the ridge have swallowed up the sun,
And in one angry streak his blood has run
To left and right along the horizon dim.

There comes a buzzing plane: and now, it seems
Flies straight into the moon. Lo! where he steers
Across the pallid globe and surely nears
In that white land some harbour of dear dreams!

False, mocking fancy! Once I too could dream,
Who now can only see with vulgar eye
That he's no nearer to the moon than I
And she's a stone that catches the sun's beam.

What call have I to dream of anything?
I am a wolf. Back to the world again,
And speech of fellow-brutes that once were men
Our throats can bark for slaughter: cannot sing.

The Anti-Romantics

WHEN THEY WERE LET IN they found three young men, all very thin and pale, seated by a stove under the low roof of the hut. There was some sacking on a bench along one wall and little comfort else.

"You will fare badly here," said one of the three men. "But I am a Steward and it is my duty according to my office to share my supper with you. You may come in." His name was Mr. Neo-Angular.

"I am sorry that my convictions do not allow me to repeat my friend's offer," said one of the others. "But I have had to abandon the humanitarian and egalitarian fallacies." His name was Mr. Neo-Classical.

"I hope," said the third, "that your wanderings in lonely places do not mean that you have any of the romantic virus still in your blood," His name was Mr. Humanist.

John was too tired and Drudge too respectful to reply: but Vertue said to Mr. Neo-Angular. "You are very kind. You are saving our lives."

"I am not kind at all," said Mr. Neo-Angular with some warmth. "I am doing my duty. My ethics are based on dogma, not on feeling."

"I understand you very well," said Vertue. "May I shake hands with you?"

"Can it be," said the other, "that you are one of us? You are a Catholic? A scholastic?"

"I know nothing about that," said Vertue, "but I know that the rule is to be obeyed because it is a rule and not because it appeals to my feelings at the moment."

"I see you are not one of us," said Angular, "and you are undoubtedly damned. *Virtutes paganorum splendida vitia.* Now let us eat."

Then I dreamed that the three pale men produced three tins of bully beef and six biscuits, and Angular shared his with the guests. There was very little for each and I thought that the best share fell to John and Drudge, for Vertue and the young Steward entered into a kind of rivalry who should leave most for the others.

"Our fare is simple," said Mr. Neo-Classical. "And perhaps unwelcome to palates that have been reared on the kickshaws of lower countries. But you see the perfection of form. This beef is a perfect cube: this biscuit a true square."

"You will admit," said Mr. Humanist, "that, at least, our meal is quite free from any lingering flavour of the old romantic sauces."

Modern Music

GLUGLY INSTANTLY ROSE. She was very tall and as lean as a post: and her mouth was not quite straight in her face. When she was in the middle of the room, and silence had been obtained, she began to make gestures. First of all she set her arms a-kimbo and cleverly turned her hands the wrong way so that it looked as if her wrists were sprained. Then she waddled to and fro with her toes pointing in. After that she twisted herself to make it look as if her hip bone was out of joint. Finally she made some grunts, and said:

"Globol obol oogle ogle globol gloogle gloo," and ended by pursing up her lips and making a vulgar noise such as children make in their nurseries. Then she went back to her place and sat down.

"Thank you very much," said John politely.

But Glugly made no reply, for Glugly could not talk, owing to an accident in infancy.

"I hoped you liked it," said young Halfways.

"I didn't understand her."

"Ah," said a woman in spectacles who seemed to be Glugly's nurse or keeper, "that is because you are looking for beauty. You are still thinking of your Island. You have got to realize that satire is the moving force in modern music."

"It is the expression of a savage disillusionment," said someone else.

"Reality has broken down," said a fat boy who had drunk a great deal of the medicine and was lying flat on his back, smiling happily.

"Our art *must* be brutal," said Glugly's nurse.

"We lost our ideals when there was a war in this country," said a very young Clever, "they were ground out of us in the mud and the flood and the blood. That is why we have to be so stark and brutal."

"But, look here," cried John, "that was years ago. It was your fathers who were in it: and they are all settled down and living ordinary lives."

"Puritanian! Bourgeois!" cried the Clevers. Everyone seemed to have risen.

"Hold your tongue," whispered Gus in John's ear. But already someone had struck John on the head, and as he bowed under the blow someone else hit him from behind.

"It was the mud and the blood," hissed the girls all round him.

"Well," said John, ducking to avoid a retort that had been flung at him, "if you are really old enough to remember that war, why do you pretend to be so young?"

"We are young," they howled; "we are the new movement; we are the revolt."

"We have got over humanitarianism," bellowed one of the bearded men, kicking John on the kneecap.

"And prudery," said a thin little old maid trying to wrench his clothes off from the neck. And at the same moment six girls leaped at his face with their nails, and he was kicked in the back and the belly, and tripped up so that he fell on his face, and hit again as he rose, and all the glass in the world seemed breaking round his head as he fled for his life from the laboratory. And all the dogs of Eschropolis joined in the chase as he ran along the street, and all the people followed pelting him with ordure, and crying:

"Puritanian! Bourgeois! Prurient."

Modern Poetry

GUS HALFWAYS WAS THE NAME of Mr. Halfways' son. As soon as he rose in the morning he called John down to breakfast with him so that they might start on their journey. There was no one to hinder them, for old Halfways was still asleep and Media always had breakfast in bed. When they had eaten, Gus brought him into a shed beside his father's house and showed him a machine on wheels.

"What is this?" said John.

"My old bus," said young Halfways. Then he stood back with his head on one side and gazed at it for a bit; but presently he began to speak in a changed and reverent voice.

"She is a poem. She is the daughter of the spirit of the age. What was the speed of Atalanta to her speed? The beauty of Apollo to her beauty?"

Now beauty to John meant nothing save glimpses of his Island, and the machine did not remind him of his Island at all: so he held his tongue.

"Don't you see?" said Gus. "Our fathers made images of what they called gods and goddesses; but they were really only brown girls and brown boys whitewashed—as anyone found out by looking at them too long. All self-deception and phallic sentiment. But here you have the real art. Nothing erotic about *her*, eh?"

"Certainly not," said John, looking at the cog-wheels and coils of wire, "it is certainly not at all like a brown girl." It was, in fact, more like a nest of hedgehogs and serpents.

"I should say not," said Gus. "Sheer power, eh? Speed, ruthlessness, austerity, significant form, eh? Also" (and here he dropped his voice) "very expensive indeed."

Then he made John sit in the machine and he himself sat beside him. Then he began pulling the levers about and for a long time nothing happened; but at last there came a flash and a roar and the machine bounded into the air and then dashed forward. Before John had got his breath they had flashed across a broad thoroughfare which he recognized as the main road, and were racing through the country to the north of it—a flat country of square stony fields divided by barbed wire fences. A moment later they were standing still in a city where all the houses were built of steel.

Modern Poetry

A CONFESSION

I am so coarse, the things the poets see
Are obstinately invisible to me.
For twenty years I've stared my level best
To see if evening—any evening—would suggest
A patient etherized upon a table;
In vain. I simply wasn't able.
To me each evening looked far more
Like the departure from a silent, yet a crowded, shore
Of a ship whose freight was everything, leaving behind
Gracefully, finally, without farewells, marooned mankind.

Red dawn behind a hedgerow in the east
Never, for me, resembled in the least
A chilblain on a cocktail-shaker's nose;
Waterfalls don't remind me of torn underclothes,
Nor glaciers of tin-cans. I've never known
The moon look like a hump-backed crone—
Rather, a prodigy, even now
Not naturalized, a riddle glaring from the Cyclops' brow
Of the cold world, reminding me on what a place
I crawl and cling, a planet with no bulwarks, out in space.

Never the white sun of the wintriest day
Struck me as *un crachat d'estaminet*.
I'm like that odd man Wordsworth knew, to whom
A primrose was a yellow primrose, one whose doom
Keeps him forever in the list of dunces,
Compelled to live on stock responses,
Making the poor best that I can

Of dull things . . . peacocks, honey, the Great Wall,
    Aldebaran,
Silver weirs, new-cut grass, wave on the beach, hard gem,
The shapes of horse and woman, Athens, Troy, Jerusalem.

Thirst and the Lion

JILL GOT UP and looked round her very carefully. There was
no sign of the Lion; but there were so many trees about that
it might easily be quite close without her seeing it. For all
she knew, there might be several lions. But her thirst was
very bad now, and she plucked up her courage to go and
look for that running water. She went on tiptoes, stealing
cautiously from tree to tree, and stopping to peer round her
at every step.

The wood was so still that it was not difficult to decide
where the sound was coming from. It grew clearer every
moment and, sooner than she expected, she came to an
open glade and saw the stream, bright as glass, running
across the turf a stone's throw away from her. But although
the sight of the water made her feel ten times thirstier than
before, she didn't rush forward and drink. She stood as still
as if she had been turned into stone, with her mouth wide
open. And she had a very good reason: just on this side of
the stream lay the Lion.

It lay with its head raised and its two fore-paws out in
front of it, like the lions in Trafalgar Square. She knew at
once that it had seen her, for its eyes looked straight into
hers for a moment and then turned away—as if it knew her
quite well and didn't think much of her.

"If I run away, it'll be after me in a moment," thought
Jill. "And if I go on, I shall run straight into its mouth."
Anyway, she couldn't have moved if she had tried, and she

couldn't take her eyes off it. How long this lasted, she could not be sure; it seemed like hours. And the thirst became so bad that she almost felt she would not mind being eaten by the Lion if only she could be sure of getting a mouthful of water first.

"If you're thirsty, you may drink."

They were the first words she had heard since Scrubb had spoken to her on the edge of the cliff. For a second she stared here and there, wondering who had spoken. Then the voice said again, "If you are thirsty, come and drink," and of course she remembered what Scrubb had said about animals talking in that other world, and realised that it was the Lion speaking. Anyway, she had seen its lips move this time, and the voice was not like a man's. It was deeper, wilder, and stronger; a sort of heavy, golden voice. It did not make her any less frightened than she had been before, but it made her frightened in rather a different way.

"Are you not thirsty?" said the Lion.

"I'm *dying* of thirst," said Jill.

"Then drink," said the Lion.

"May I—could I—would you mind going away while I do?" said Jill.

The Lion answered this only by a look and a very low growl. And as Jill gazed at its motionless bulk, she realised that she might as well have asked the whole mountain to move aside for her convenience.

The delicious rippling noise of the stream was driving her nearly frantic.

"Will you promise not to—do anything to me, if I do come?" said Jill.

"I make no promise," said the Lion.

Jill was so thirsty now that, without noticing it, she had come a step nearer.

"*Do* you eat girls?" she said.

"I have swallowed up girls and boys, women and men, kings and emperors, cities and realms," said the Lion. It didn't say this as if it were boasting, nor as if it were sorry, nor as if it were angry. It just said it.

"I daren't come and drink," said Jill.

"Then you will die of thirst," said the Lion.

"Oh dear!" said Jill, coming another step nearer. "I suppose I must go and look for another stream then."

"There is no other stream," said the Lion.

It never occurred to Jill to disbelieve the Lion—no one who had seen his stern face could do that—and her mind suddenly made itself up. It was the worst thing she had ever had to do, but she went forward to the stream, knelt down, and began scooping up water in her hand. It was the coldest, most refreshing water she had ever tasted. You didn't need to drink much of it, for it quenched your thirst at once. Before she tasted it she had been intending to make a dash away from the Lion the moment she had finished. Now, she realised that this would be on the whole the most dangerous thing of all. She got up and stood there with her lips still wet from drinking.

"Come here," said the Lion. And she had to. She was almost between its front paws now, looking straight into its face. But she couldn't stand that for long; she dropped her eyes.

Feasting with the Lamb

As THE SUN ROSE the sight of those mountains outside the world faded away. The wave remained but there was only blue sky behind it.

The children got out of the boat and waded—not towards the wave but southward with the wall of water on their left. They could not have told you why they did this; it was their fate. And though they had felt—and been—very grown up on the *Dawn Treader,* they now felt just the opposite and held hands as they waded through the lilies. They never felt tired. The water was warm and all the time it got shallower. At last they were on dry sand, and then on grass—a huge plain of very fine short grass, almost level with the Silver Sea and spreading in every direction without so much as a molehill.

And of course, as it always does in a perfectly flat place without trees, it looked as if the sky came down to meet the grass in front of them. But as they went on they got the strangest impression that here at last the sky did really come down and join the earth—a blue wall, very bright, but real and solid, more like glass than anything else. And soon they were quite sure of it. It was very near now.

But between them and the foot of the sky there was something so white on the green grass that even with their eagles' eyes they could hardly look at it. They came on and saw that it was a Lamb.

"Come and have breakfast," said the Lamb in its sweet milky voice.

Then they noticed for the first time that there was a fire lit on the grass and fish roasting on it. They sat down and ate the fish, hungry now for the first time for many days. And it was the most delicious food they had ever tasted.

"Please, Lamb," said Lucy, "is this the way to Aslan's country?"

"Not for you," said the Lamb. "For you the door into Aslan's country is from your own world."

"What!" said Edmund. "Is there a way into Aslan's country from our world too?"

"There is a way into my country from all the worlds," said the Lamb; but as he spoke his snowy white flushed into tawny gold and his size changed and he was Aslan himself, towering above them and scattering light from his mane.

"Oh, Aslan," said Lucy. "Will you tell us how to get into your country from our world?"

"I shall be telling you all the time," said Aslan. "But I will not tell you how long or short the way will be; only that it lies across a river. But do not fear that, for I am the great Bridge Builder. And now come; I will open the door in the sky and send you to your own land."

"Please, Aslan," said Lucy. "Before we go, will you tell us when we can come back to Narnia again? Please. And oh, do, do, do make it soon."

"Dearest," said Aslan very gently, "you and your brother will never come back to Narnia."

"Oh, *Aslan!*" said Edmund and Lucy both together in despairing voices.

"You are too old, children," said Aslan, "and you must begin to come close to your own world now."

"It isn't Narnia, you know," sobbed Lucy. "It's *you*. We shan't meet *you* there. And how can we live, never meeting you?"

"But you shall meet me, dear one," said Aslan.

"Are—are you there too, Sir?" said Edmund.

"I am," said Aslan. "But there I have another name. You must learn to know me by that name. This was the very reason why you were brought to Narnia, that by knowing me here for a little, you may know me better there."

Creation

IN A FEW MINUTES Digory came to the edge of the wood and there he stopped. The Lion was singing still. But now the song had once more changed. It was more like what we should call a tune, but it was also far wilder. It made you want to run and jump and climb. It made you want to shout. It made you want to rush at other people and either hug them or fight them. It made Digory hot and red in the face. It had some effect even on Uncle Andrew, for Digory could hear him saying, "A spirited gel, sir. It's a pity about her temper, but a dem fine woman all the same, a dem fine woman." But what the song did to the two humans was nothing compared with what it was doing to the country.

Can you imagine a stretch of grassy land bubbling like water in a pot? For that is really the best description of what was happening. In all directions it was swelling into humps. They were of very different sizes, some no bigger than mole-hills, some as big as wheel-barrows, two the size of cottages. And the humps moved and swelled till they burst, and the crumbled earth poured out of them, and from each hump there came out an animal. The moles came out just as you might see a mole come out in England. The dogs came out, barking the moment their heads were free, and struggling as you've seen them do when they are getting through a narrow hole in a hedge. The stags were the queerest to watch, for of course the antlers came up a long time before the rest of them, so at first Digory thought they were trees. The frogs, who all came up near the river, went straight into it with a plop-plop and a loud croaking. The panthers, leopards and things of that sort, sat down at once to wash the loose earth off their hind quarters and then stood up against the trees to sharpen their front claws. Showers of birds came out of the trees. Butterflies fluttered. Bees got to work on the flowers as if they hadn't a second to lose. But the greatest moment of all was when the biggest hump broke like a small earthquake and out came the sloping back, the large, wise head, and the four baggy trousered legs of an Elephant. And now you could hardly hear the song of the Lion; there was so much cawing, cooing, crowing, braying, neighing, baying, barking, lowing, bleating, and trumpeting.

But though Digory could no longer hear the Lion, he could see it. It was so big and so bright that he could not take his eyes off it. The other animals did not appear to be afraid of it. Indeed, at that very moment, Digory heard the sound of hoofs from behind; a second later the old cab-horse trotted past him and joined the other beasts. (The air had apparently suited him as well as it had suited Uncle Andrew. He no longer looked like the poor, old slave he had been in London; he was picking up his feet and holding his head erect.) And now, for the first time, the Lion was quite silent. He was going to and fro among the animals. And every now and then he would go up to two of them (always two at a time) and touch their noses with his. He would touch two beavers among all the beavers, two leopards among all the leopards, one stag and one deer among all the deer, and leave the rest. Some sorts of animal he passed over altogether. But the pairs which he had touched instantly left their own kinds and followed him. At last he stood still and all the creatures whom he had touched came and stood in a wide circle around him. The others whom he had not touched began to wander away. Their noises faded gradually into the distance. The chosen beasts who remained were now utterly silent, all with their eyes fixed intently upon the Lion. The cat-like ones gave an occasional twitch of the tail but otherwise all were still. For the first time that day there was complete silence, except for the noise of running water. Digory's heart beat wildly; he knew something very solemn was going to be done. He had not forgotten about his Mother; but he knew jolly well that, even for her, he couldn't interrupt a thing like this.

The Lion, whose eyes never blinked, stared at the animals as hard as if he was going to burn them up with his mere stare. And gradually a change came over them. The smaller ones—the rabbits, moles and such-like—grew a good deal larger. The very big ones—you noticed it most with the elephants—grew a little smaller. Many animals sat up on their hind legs. Most put their heads on one side as if they were trying very hard to understand. The Lion opened his mouth, but no sound came from it; he was breathing out, a long, warm breath; it seemed to sway all the beasts as the wind sways a line of trees. Far overhead from beyond the veil of blue sky which hid them the stars sang again: a pure, cold, difficult music. Then there came a swift flash like fire (but it burnt nobody) either from the sky or from the Lion itself, and every drop of blood tingled in the children's bodies, and the deepest, wildest voice they had ever heard was saying:

"Narnia, Narnia, Narnia, awake. Love. Think. Speak. Be walking trees. Be talking beasts. Be divine waters."

The Agony of Aslan

VERY QUIETLY the two girls groped their way among the other sleepers and crept out of the tent. The moonlight was bright and everything was quite still except for the noise of the river chattering over the stones. Then Susan suddenly caught Lucy's arm and said, "Look!" On the far side of the camping ground, just where the trees began, they saw the Lion slowly walking away from them into the wood. Without a word they both followed him.

He led them up the steep slope out of the river valley and then slightly to the left—apparently by the very same route which they had used that afternoon in coming from the Hill of the Stone Table. On and on he led them, into dark shadows and out into pale moonlight, getting their feet wet with the heavy dew. He looked somehow different from the Aslan they knew. His tail and his head hung low and he walked slowly as if he were very, very tired. Then, when they were crossing a wide open place where there were no shadows for them to hide in, he stopped and looked round. It was no good trying to run away so they came towards him. When they were closer he said,

"Oh, children, children, why are you following me?"

"We couldn't sleep," said Lucy—and then felt sure that she need say no more and that Aslan knew all they had been thinking.

"Please, may we come with you—wherever you're going?" said Susan.

"Well—" said Aslan and seemed to be thinking. Then he said, "I should be glad of company to-night. Yes, you may come, if you will promise to stop when I tell you, and after that leave me to go on alone."

"Oh, thank you, thank you. And we will," said the two girls.

Forward they went again and one of the girls walked on each side of the Lion. But how slowly he walked! And his great, royal head drooped so that his nose nearly touched the grass. Presently he stumbled and gave a low moan.

"Aslan! Dear Aslan!" said Lucy, "what is wrong? Can't you tell us?"

"Are you ill, dear Aslan?" asked Susan.

"No," said Aslan. "I am sad and lonely. Lay your hands on my mane so that I can feel you are there and let us walk like that."

And so the girls did what they would never have dared to do without his permission but what they had longed to do ever since they first saw him—buried their cold hands in the beautiful sea of fur and stroked it and, so doing, walked with him. And presently they saw that they were going with him up the slope of the hill on which the Stone Table stood. They went up at the side where the trees came furthest up, and when they got to the last tree (it was one that had some bushes about it) Aslan stopped and said,

"Oh, children, children. Here you must stop. And whatever happens, do not let yourselves be seen. Farewell."

Atonement

AND BOTH THE GIRLS cried bitterly (though they hardly knew why) and clung to the Lion and kissed his mane and his nose and his paws and his great, sad eyes. Then he turned from them and walked out onto the top of the hill. And Lucy and Susan, crouching in the bushes, looked after him and this is what they saw.

A great crowd of people were standing all round the Stone Table and though the moon was shining many of them carried torches which burned with evil-looking red flames and black smoke. But such people! Ogres with monstrous teeth, and wolves, and bull-headed men; spirits of evil trees and poisonous plants; and other creatures whom I won't describe because if I did the grown-ups would probably not let you read this book—Cruels and Hags and Incubuses, Wraiths, Horrors, Efreets, Sprites, Orknies, Wooses, and Ettins. In fact here were all those who were on the Witch's side and whom the Wolf had summoned at her command. And right in the middle, standing by the Table, was the Witch herself.

A howl and a gibber of dismay went up from the creatures when they first saw the great Lion pacing towards them, and for a moment the Witch herself seemed to be struck with fear. Then she recovered herself and gave a wild, fierce laugh.

"The fool!" she cried. "The fool has come. Bind him fast."

Lucy and Susan held their breaths waiting for Aslan's roar and his spring upon his enemies. But it never came. Four hags, grinning and leering, yet also (at first) hanging back and half afraid of what they had to do, had approached him. "Bind him, I say!" repeated the White

Witch. The hags made a dart at him and shrieked with triumph when they found that he made no resistance at all. Then others—evil dwarfs and apes—rushed in to help them and between them they rolled the huge Lion round on his back and tied all his four paws together, shouting and cheering as if they had done something brave, though, had the Lion chosen, one of those paws could have been the death of them all. But he made no noise, even when the enemies, straining and tugging, pulled the cords so tight that they cut into his flesh. Then they began to drag him towards the Stone Table.

"Stop!" said the Witch. "Let him first be shaved."

Another roar of mean laughter went up from her followers as an ogre with a pair of shears came forward and squatted down by Aslan's head. Snip-snip-snip went the shears and masses of curling gold began to fall to the ground. Then the ogre stood back and the children, watching from their hiding-place, could see the face of Aslan looking all small and different without its mane. The enemies also saw the difference.

"Why, he's only a great cat after all!" cried one.

"Is *that* what we were afraid of?" said another.

And they surged round Aslan jeering at him, saying things like "Puss, Puss! Poor Pussy," and "How many mice have you caught to-day, Cat?" and "Would you like a saucer of milk, Pussums?"

"Oh how *can* they?" said Lucy, tears streaming down her cheeks. "The brutes, the brutes!" For now that the first shock was over the shorn face of Aslan looked to her braver, and more beautiful, and more patient than ever.

"Muzzle him!" said the Witch. And even now, as they worked about his face putting on the muzzle, one bite from his jaws would have cost two or three of them their hands. But he never moved. And this seemed to enrage all that rabble. Everyone was at him now. Those who had been afraid to come near him even after he was bound began to find their courage, and for a few minutes the two girls could not even see him—so thickly was he surrounded by the whole crowd of creatures kicking him, hitting him, spitting on him, jeering at him.

At last the rabble had had enough of this. They began to drag the bound and muzzled Lion to the Stone Table, some pulling and some pushing. He was so huge that even when they got him there it took all their efforts to hoist him onto the surface of it. Then there was more tying and tightening of cords.

"The cowards! The cowards!" sobbed Susan. "Are they *still* afraid of him, even now?"

When once Aslan had been tied (and tied so that he was really a mass of cords) on the flat stone, a hush fell on the crowd. Four Hags, holding four torches, stood at the corners of the Table. The Witch bared her arms as she had bared them the previous night when it had been Edmund instead of Aslan. Then she began to whet her knife. It looked to the children, when the gleam of the torchlight fell on it, as if the knife were made of stone not of steel and it was of a strange and evil shape.

At last she drew near. She stood by Aslan's head. Her face was working and twitching with passion, but his looked up at the sky, still quiet, neither angry nor afraid, but a little sad. Then, just before she gave the blow, she stooped down and said in a quivering voice,

"And now, who has won? Fool, did you think that by all this you would save the human traitor? Now I will kill you instead of him as our pact was and so the Deep Magic will be appeased. But when you are dead what will prevent me from killing him as well? And who will take him out of my hand *then*? Understand that you have given me Narnia forever, you have lost your own life and you have not saved his. In that knowledge, despair and die."

The children did not see the actual moment of the killing. They couldn't bear to look and had covered their eyes.

Resurrection

THE RISING OF THE SUN had made everything look so different—all the colours and shadows were changed—that for a
moment they didn't see the important thing. Then they did.
The Stone Table was broken into two pieces by a great crack
that ran down it from end to end; and there was no Aslan.

"Oh, oh, oh!" cried the two girls rushing back to the
Table.

"Oh, it's *too* bad," sobbed Lucy; "they might have left
the body alone."

"Who's done it?" cried Susan. "What does it mean? Is it
more magic?"

"Yes!" said a great voice behind their backs. "It is more
magic." They looked round. There, shining in the sunrise,
larger than they had seen him before, shaking his mane (for
it had apparently grown again) stood Aslan himself.

"Oh, Aslan!" cried both the children, staring up at him,
almost as much frightened as they were glad.

"Aren't you dead then, dear Aslan?" said Lucy.

"Not now," said Aslan.

"You're not—not a—?" asked Susan in a shaky voice. She
couldn't bring herself to say the word *ghost*.

Aslan stooped his golden head and licked her forehead.
The warmth of his breath and a rich sort of smell that
seemed to hang about his hair came all over her.

"Do I look it?" he said.

"Oh, you're real, you're real! Oh, Aslan!" cried Lucy and
both girls flung themselves upon him and covered him with
kisses.

"But what does it all mean?" asked Susan when they
were somewhat calmer.

"It means," said Aslan, "that though the Witch knew the

Deep Magic, there is a magic deeper still which she did not know. Her knowledge goes back only to the dawn of Time. But if she could have looked a little further back, into the stillness and the darkness before Time dawned, she would have read there a different incantation. She would have known that when a willing victim who had committed no treachery was killed in a traitor's stead, the Table would crack and Death itself would start working backwards. And now—"

"Oh yes. Now?" said Lucy jumping up and clapping her hands.

"Oh, children," said the Lion, "I feel my strength coming back to me. Oh, children, catch me if you can!" He stood for a second, his eyes very bright, his limbs quivering, lashing himself with his tail. Then he made a leap high over their heads and landed on the other side of the Table. Laughing, though she didn't know why, Lucy scrambled over it to reach him. Aslan leaped again. A mad chase began. Round and round the hill-top he led them, now hopelessly out of their reach, now letting them almost catch his tail, now diving between them, now tossing them in the air with his huge and beautifully velveted paws and catching them again, and now stopping unexpectedly so that all three of them rolled over together in a happy laughing heap of fur and arms and legs. It was such a romp as no one has ever had except in Narnia; and whether it was more like playing with a thunderstorm or playing with a kitten Lucy could never make up her mind. And the funny thing was that when all three finally lay together panting in the sun the girls no longer felt in the least tired or hungry or thirsty.

"And now," said Aslan presently, "to business. I feel I am going to roar. You had better put your fingers in your ears."

And they did. And Aslan stood up and when he opened his mouth to roar his face became so terrible that they did not dare to look at it. And they saw all the trees in front of him bend before the blast of his roaring as grass bends in a meadow before the wind. Then he said,

"We have a long journey to go. You must ride on me." And he crouched down and the children climbed onto his warm, golden back and Susan sat first holding on tightly to his mane and Lucy sat behind holding on tightly to Susan. And with a great heave he rose underneath them and then shot off, faster than any horse could go, downhill and into the thick of the forest.

Last Things

THEN THE GREAT GIANT raised a horn to his mouth. They could see this by the change of the black shape he made against the stars. After that—quite a bit later, because sound travels so slowly—they heard the sound of the horn: high and terrible, yet of a strange, deadly beauty.

Immediately the sky became full of shooting stars. Even one shooting star is a fine thing to see; but these were dozens, and then scores, and then hundreds, till it was like silver rain: and it went on and on. And when it had gone on for some while, one or two of them began to think that there was another dark shape against the sky as well as the giant's. It was in a different place, right overhead, up in the very roof of the sky as you might call it. "Perhaps it is a cloud," thought Edmund. At any rate, there were no stars there: just blackness. But all around, the downpour of stars went on. And then the starless patch began to grow, spreading further and further out from the centre of the sky. And presently a quarter of the whole sky was black, and then a half, and at last the rain of shooting stars was going on only low down near the horizon.

With a thrill of wonder (and there was some terror in it

too) they all suddenly realized what was happening. The spreading blackness was not a cloud at all: it was simply emptiness. The black part of the sky was the part in which there were no stars left. All the stars were falling: Aslan had called them home.

The last few seconds before the rain of stars had quite ended were very exciting. Stars began falling all round them. But stars in that world are not the great flaming globes they are in ours. They are people (Edmund and Lucy had once met one). So now they found showers of glittering people, all with long hair like burning silver and spears like white-hot metal, rushing down to them out of the black air, swifter than falling stones. They made a hissing noise as they landed and burnt the grass. And all these stars glided past them and stood somewhere behind, a little to the right.

This was a great advantage, because otherwise, now that there were no stars in the sky, everything would have been completely dark and you could have seen nothing. As it was, the crowd of stars behind them cast a fierce, white light over their shoulders. They could see mile upon mile of Narnian woods spread out before them, looking as if they were flood-lit. Every bush and almost every blade of grass had its black shadow behind it. The edge of every leaf stood out so sharp that you'd think you could cut your finger on it.

On the grass before them lay their own shadows. But the great thing was Aslan's shadow. It streamed away to their left, enormous and very terrible. And all this was under a sky that would now be starless for ever.

The light from behind them (and a little to their right) was so strong that it lit up even the slopes of the Northern Moors. Something was moving there. Enormous animals were crawling and sliding down into Narnia: great dragons and giant lizards and featherless birds with wings like bats' wings. They disappeared into the woods and for a few minutes there was silence. Then there came—at first from very far off—sounds of wailing and then, from every direction, a rustling and a pattering and a sound of wings. It came nearer and nearer. Soon one could distinguish the scamper of little feet from the padding of big paws, and the clack-clack of light little hoofs from the thunder of great ones. And then one could see thousands of pairs of eyes gleaming. And at last, out of the shadow of the trees, racing up the hill for dear life, by thousands and by millions, came all kinds of creatures—Talking Beasts, Dwarfs, Satyrs, Fauns, Giants, Calormenes, men from Archenland, Monopods, and strange unearthly things from the remote islands or the unknown Western lands. And all these ran up to the doorway where Aslan stood.

This part of the adventure was the only one which seemed rather like a dream at the time and rather hard to remember properly afterwards. Especially, one couldn't say how long it had taken. Sometimes it seemed to have lasted only a few minutes, but at others it felt as if it might have gone on for years. Obviously, unless either the Door had grown very much larger or the creatures had suddenly grown as small as gnats, a crowd like that couldn't ever have tried to get through it. But no one thought about that sort of thing at the time.

The creatures came rushing on, their eyes brighter and brighter as they drew nearer and nearer to the standing Stars. But as they came right up to Aslan one or other of two things happened to each of them. They all looked straight in his face; I don't think they had any choice about that. And when some looked, the expression of their faces changed terribly—it was fear and hatred: except that, on the faces of Talking Beasts, the fear and hatred lasted only for a fraction of a second. You could see that they suddenly ceased to be *Talking* Beasts. They were just ordinary animals. And all the creatures who looked at Aslan in that way swerved to their right, his left, and disappeared into his huge black shadow, which (as you have heard) streamed away to the left of the doorway. The children never saw them again. I don't know what became of them. But the others looked in the face of Aslan and loved him, though some of them were very frightened at the same time. And all these came in at the Door, in on Aslan's right. There were some queer specimens among them. Eustace even recognised one of those very Dwarfs who had helped to shoot the Horses. But he had no time to wonder about that sort of thing (and anyway it was no business of his) for a great joy put everything else out of his head. Among the happy creatures who now came crowding round Tirian and his friends were all those whom they had thought dead. There was Roonwit the Centaur and Jewel the Unicorn, and the good Boar and the good Bear and Farsight the Eagle, and the dear Dogs and the Horses, and Poggin the Dwarf.

New Things

"THE EAGLE is right," said the Lord Digory. "Listen, Peter. When Aslan said you could never go back to Narnia, he meant the Narnia you were thinking of. But that was not the real Narnia. That had a beginning and an end. It was only a shadow or a copy of the real Narnia, which has always been here and always will be here: just as our own world, England and all, is only a shadow or copy of something in Aslan's real world. You need not mourn over Narnia, Lucy. All of the old Narnia that mattered, all the dear creatures, have been drawn into the real Narnia through the Door. And of course it is different; as different as a real thing is from a shadow or as waking life is from a dream." His voice stirred everyone like a trumpet as he spoke these words: but when he added under his breath "It's all in Plato, all in Plato: bless me, what *do* they teach them at these schools!'' the older ones laughed. It was so exactly like the sort of thing they had heard him say long ago in that other world where his beard was grey instead of golden. He knew why they were laughing and joined in the laugh himself. But very quickly they all became grave again: for, as you know, there is a kind of happiness and wonder that makes you serious. It is too good to waste on jokes.

It is as hard to explain how this sunlit land was different from the old Narnia, as it would be to tell you how the fruits of that country taste. Perhaps you will get some idea of it, if you think like this. You may have been in a room in which there was a window that looked out on a lovely bay of the sea or a green valley that wound away among mountains. And in the wall of that room opposite to the window there may have been a looking glass. And as you turned away from the window you suddenly caught sight of that sea or that valley, all over again, in the looking glass. And the sea in the mirror, or the valley in the mirror, were in one sense just the same as the real ones: yet at the same time they were somehow different—deeper, more wonderful, more like places in a story: in a story you have never heard but very much want to know. The difference between the old Narnia and the new Narnia was like that. The new one was a deeper country: every rock and flower and blade of grass looked as if it meant more. I can't describe it any better than that: if you ever get there, you will know what I mean.

New Life

EVERY MOMENT the patches of green grew bigger and the patches of snow grew smaller. Every moment more and more of the trees shook off their robes of snow. Soon, wherever you looked, instead of white shapes you saw the dark green of firs or the black prickly branches of bare oaks and beeches and elms. Then the mist turned from white to gold and presently cleared away altogether. Shafts of delicious sunlight struck down onto the forest floor and overhead you could see a blue sky between the tree-tops.

Soon there were more wonderful things happening. Coming suddenly round a corner into a glade of silver birch trees Edmund saw the ground covered in all directions with little yellow flowers—celandines. The noise of water grew louder. Presently they actually crossed a stream. Beyond it they found snowdrops growing.

"Mind your own business!" said the Dwarf when he saw that Edmund had turned his head to look at them; and he gave the rope a vicious jerk.

But of course this didn't prevent Edmund from seeing. Only five minutes later he noticed a dozen crocuses growing round the foot of an old tree—gold and purple and white. Then came a sound even more delicious than the sound of the water. Close beside the path they were following a bird suddenly chirped from the branch of a tree. It was answered by the chuckle of another bird a little further off. And then, as if that had been a signal, there was chattering and chirruping in every direction, and then a moment of full song, and within five minutes the whole wood was ringing with birds' music, and wherever Edmund's eyes turned he saw birds alighting on branches, or sailing overhead or having their little quarrels.

"Faster! Faster!" said the Witch.

There was no trace of the fog now. The sky became bluer and bluer and now there were white clouds hurrying across it from time to time. In the wide glades there were primroses. A light breeze sprang up which scattered drops of moisture from the swaying branches and carried cool, delicious scents against the faces of the travellers. The trees began to come fully alive. The larches and birches were covered with green, the laburnums with gold. Soon the beech trees had put forth their delicate, transparent leaves. As the travellers walked under them the light also became green. A bee buzzed across their path.

"This is no thaw," said the Dwarf, suddenly stopping. "This is *spring*. What are we to do? Your winter has been destroyed, I tell you! This is Aslan's doing."

"If either of you mention that name again," said the Witch, "he shall instantly be killed."

The Salvation of a Pagan

"So I WENT OVER much grass and many flowers and among all kinds of wholesome and delectable trees till lo! in a narrow place between two rocks there came to meet me a great Lion. The speed of him was like the ostrich, and his size was an elephant's; his hair was like pure gold and the brightness of his eyes, like gold that is liquid in the furnace. He was more terrible than the Flaming Mountain of Lagour, and in beauty he surpassed all that is in the world, even as the rose in bloom surpasses the dust of the desert. Then I fell at his feet and thought, Surely this is the hour of death, for the Lion (who is worthy of all honour) will know that I have served Tash all my days and not him. Nevertheless, it is better to see the Lion and die than to be Tisroc of the world and live and not to have seen him. But the Glorious One bent down his golden head and touched my forehead with his tongue and said, Son, thou art welcome. But I said, Alas, Lord, I am no son of Thine but the servant of Tash. He answered, Child, all the service thou hast done to Tash, I account as service done to me. Then by reason of my great desire for wisdom and understanding, I overcame my fear and questioned the Glorious One and said, Lord, is it then true, as the Ape said, that thou and Tash are one? The Lion growled so that the earth shook (but his wrath was not against me) and said, It is false. Not because he and I are one, but because we are opposites, I take to me the services which thou hast done to him, for I and he are of such different kinds that no service which is vile can be done to me, and none which is not vile can be done to him. Therefore if any man swear by Tash and keep his oath for the oath's sake, it is by me that he has truly sworn, though he know it not, and it is I who reward him. And if any man do a cruelty in my name, then though he says the name Aslan, it is Tash whom he serves and by Tash his deed is accepted. Dost thou understand, Child? I said, Lord, thou knowest how much I understand. But I said also (for the truth constrained me), Yes I have been seeking Tash all my days. Beloved, said the Glorious One, unless thy desire had been for me thou wouldst not have sought so long and so truly. For all find what they truly seek.

Judgment

"UNCOVER HER," said the judge.

Hands came from behind me and tore off my veil—after it, every rag I had on. The old crone with her Ungit face stood naked before those countless gazers. No thread to cover me, no bowl in my hand to hold the water of death; only my book.

"Read your complaint," said the judge.

I looked at the roll in my hand and saw at once that it was not the book I had written. It couldn't be; it was far too small. And too old—a little, shabby, crumpled thing, nothing like my great book that I had worked on all day, day after day, while Bardia was dying. I thought I would fling it down and trample on it. I'd tell them someone had stolen my complaint and slipped this thing into my hand instead. Yet I found myself unrolling it. It was written all over inside, but the hand was not like mine. It was all a vile scribble—each stroke mean and yet savage, like the snarl in my father's voice, like the ruinous faces one could make out in the Ungit stone. A great terror and loathing came over me. I said to myself, "Whatever they do to me, I will never read out this stuff. Give me back my Book." But already I heard myself reading it. And what I read out was like this:

"I know what you'll say. You will say the real gods are not at all like Ungit, and that I was shown a real god and the house of a real god and ought to know it. Hypocrites! I do know it. As if that would heal my wounds! I could have endured it if you were things like Ungit and the Shadowbrute. You know well that I never really began to hate you until Psyche began talking of her palace and her lover and her husband. Why did you lie to me? You said a brute would devour her. Well, why didn't it? I'd have wept for her and buried what was left and built her a tomb and . . . and . . . . But to steal her love from me! Can it be that you really don't understand? Do you think we mortals will find you gods easier to bear if you're beautiful? I tell you that if that's true we'll find you a thousand times worse. For then (I know what beauty does) you'll lure and entice. You'll leave us nothing; nothing that's worth our keeping or your taking. Those we love best—whoever's most worth loving—those are the very ones you'll pick out. Oh, I can see it happening, age after age, and growing worse and worse the more you reveal your beauty: the son turning his back on the mother and the bride on her groom, stolen away by this everlasting calling, calling, calling of the gods. Taken where we can't follow. It would be far better for us if you were foul and ravening. We'd rather you drank their blood than stole their hearts. We'd rather they were ours and dead than yours and made immortal. But to steal her love from me, to make her see things I couldn't see . . . oh, you'll say (you've been whispering it to me these forty years) that I'd signs enough her palace was real, could have known the truth if I'd wanted. But how could I want to know it? Tell me that. The girl was mine. What right had you to steal her away into your dreadful heights? You'll say I was jealous. Jealous of Psyche? Not while she was mine. If you'd gone the other way to work—if it was my eyes you had opened—you'd soon have seen how I would have shown her and told her and taught her and led her up to my level. But to hear a chit of a girl who had (or ought to have had) no thought in her head that I'd not put there, setting up for a seer and a prophetess and next thing to a goddess . . . how could anyone endure it? That's why I say it makes no difference whether you're fair or foul. That there should be gods at all, there's our misery and bitter wrong. There's no room for you and us in the same world. You're a tree in whose shadow we can't thrive. We want to be our own. I was my own and Psyche was mine and no one else had any right to her. Oh, you'll say you took her away into bliss and joy such as I could never have given her, and I ought to have been glad of it for her sake. Why? What should I care for some horrible, new happiness which I hadn't given her and which separated her from me? Do you think I wanted her to be happy, that way? It would have been better if I'd seen the Brute tear her in pieces before my eyes. You stole her to make her happy, did you? Why, every wheedling, smiling, catfoot rogue who lures away another man's wife or slave or dog might say the same. Dog, now. That's very much to the purpose. I'll thank you to let me feed my own; it needed no tidbits from your table. Did you ever remember whose the girl was? She was mine. *Mine.* Do you not know what the word means? Mine! You're thieves, seducers. That's my wrong. I'll not complain (not now) that you're blood-drinkers and man-eaters. I'm past that. . . ."

"Enough," said the judge.

There was utter silence all round me. And now for the first time I knew what I had been doing. While I was reading, it had, once and again, seemed strange to me that the reading took so long; for the book was a small one. Now I knew that I had been reading it over and over—perhaps a dozen times. I would have read it forever, quick as I could, starting the first word again almost before the last was out of my mouth, if the judge had not stopped me. And the voice I read it in was strange to my ears. There was given to me a certainty that this, at last, was my real voice.

There was silence in the dark assembly long enough for me to have read my book out yet again. At last the judge spoke.

"Are you answered?" he said.

"Yes," said I.

A Hostile God

ODE FOR NEW YEAR'S DAY

Woe unto you, ye sons of pain that are this day in earth,
Now cry for all your torment: now curse your hour of birth
And the fathers who begat you to a portion nothing worth.
And Thou, my own belovèd, for as brave as ere thou art,
Bow down thine head, Despoina, clasp thy pale arms over
    it,
Lie low with fast-closed eyelids, clenched teeth, enduring
    heart,
For sorrow on sorrow is coming wherein all flesh has part.
The sky above is sickening, the clouds of God's hate cover
    it,
Body and soul shall suffer beyond all word or thought,
Till the pain and noisy terror that these first years have
    wrought
Seem but the soft arising and prelude of the storm
That fiercer still and heavier with sharper lightnings fraught
Shall pour red wrath upon us over a world deform.

Thrice happy, O Despoina, were the men who were alive
In the great age and the golden age when still the cycle ran
On upward curve and easily, for then both maid and man
And beast and tree and spirit in the green earth could
    thrive.
But now one age is ending, and God calls home the stars
And looses the wheel of the ages and sends it spinning back
Amid the death of nations, and points a downward track,
And madness is come over us and great and little wars.
He has not left one valley, one isle of fresh and green
Where old friends could forgather amid the howling wreck.

It's vainly we are praying. We cannot, cannot check
The Power who slays and puts aside the beauty that has
   been.

It's truth they tell, Despoina, none hears the heart's com-
   plaining
For Nature will not pity, nor the red God lend an ear.
Yet I too have been mad in the hour of bitter paining
And lifted up my voice to God, thinking that he could hear
The curse wherewith I cursed Him because the Good was
   dead.
But lo! I am grown wiser, knowing that our own hearts
Have made a phantom called the Good, while a few years
   have sped
Over a little planet. And what should the great Lord know
   of it
Who tosses the dust of chaos and gives the suns their parts?
Hither and thither he moves them; for an hour we see the
   show of it:
Only a little hour, and the life of the race is done.
And here he builds a nebula, and there he slays a sun
And works his own fierce pleasure. All things he shall fulfil,
And O, my poor Despoina, do you think he ever hears
The wail of hearts he has broken, the sound of human ill?
He cares not for our virtues, our little hopes and fears,
And how could it all go on, love, if he knew of laughter and
   tears?

Ah, sweet, if a man could cheat him! If you could flee away
Into some other country beyond the rosy West,
To hide in the deep forests and be for ever at rest
From the rankling hate of God and the outworn world's
   decay!

God's Footprints

SONG

Faeries must be in the woods
Or the satyrs' laughing broods—
Tritons in the summer sea,
Else how could the dead things be
Half so lovely as they are?
How could wealth of star on star
Dusted o'er the frosty night
Fill thy spirit with delight
And lead thee from this care of thine
Up among the dreams divine,
Were it not that each and all
Of them that walk the heavenly hall
Is in truth a happy isle,
Where eternal meadows smile,
And golden globes of fruit are seen
Twinkling through the orchards green;
Where the Other People go
On the bright sward to and fro?
Atoms dead could never thus
Stir the human heart of us
Unless the beauty that we see
The veil of endless beauty be,
Filled full of spirits that have trod
Far hence along the heavenly sod
And seen the bright footprints of God.

Conversion

JANE HAD GONE INTO THE GARDEN to think. She accepted what the Director had said, yet it seemed to her nonsensical. His comparison between Mark's love and God's (since apparently there was a God) struck her nascent spirituality as indecent and irreverent. "Religion" ought to mean a realm in which her haunting female fear of being treated as a thing, an object of barter and desire and possession, would be set permanently at rest and what she called her "true self" would soar upwards and expand in some freer and purer world. For still she thought that "Religion" was a kind of exhalation or a cloud of incense, something steaming up from specially gifted souls towards a receptive Heaven. Then, quite sharply, it occurred to her that the Director never talked about Religion; nor did the Dimbles nor Camilla. They talked about God. They had no picture in their minds of some mist steaming upward: rather of strong, skilful hands thrust down to make, and mend, perhaps even to destroy. Supposing one were a *thing* after all—a thing designed and invented by Someone Else and valued for qualities quite different from what one had decided to regard as one's true self? Supposing all those people who, from the bachelor uncles down to Mark and Mother Dimble, had infuriatingly found her sweet and fresh when she wanted them to find her also interesting and important, had all along been simply right and perceived the sort of thing she was? Supposing Maleldil on this subject agreed with them and not with her? For one moment she had a ridiculous and scorching vision of a world in which God Himself would never understand, never take her with full seriousness. Then, at one particular corner of the gooseberry patch, the change came.

What awaited her there was serious to the degree of sorrow and beyond. There was no form nor sound. The mould under the bushes, the moss on the path, and the little brick border, were not visibly changed. But they were changed. A boundary had been crossed. She had come into a world, or into a Person, or into the presence of a Person. Something expectant, patient, inexorable, met her with no veil or protection between. In the closeness of that contact she perceived at once that the Director's words had been entirely misleading. This demand which now pressed upon her was not, even by analogy, like any other demand. It was the origin of all right demands and contained them. In its light you could understand them; but from them you could know nothing of it. There was nothing, and never had been anything, like this. And now there was nothing except this. Yet also, everything had been like this; only by being like this had anything existed. In this height and depth and breadth the little idea of herself which she had hitherto called *me* dropped down and vanished, unfluttering, into bottomless distance, like a bird in a space without air. The name *me* was the name of a being whose existence she had never suspected, a being that did not yet fully exist but which was demanded. It was a person (not the person she had thought), yet also a thing, a made thing, made to please Another and in Him to please all others, a thing being made at this very moment, without its choice, in a shape it had never dreamed of. And the making went on amidst a kind of splendour or sorrow or both, whereof she could not tell whether it was in the moulding hands or in the kneaded lump.

Encounter with God the Thou

HE WAS MUCH COMFORTED by this idea of metaphor, and as he was now also rested, he began his journey along the cliff path with some degree of timid resolution. But it was very dreadful to him in the narrower places: and his courage seemed to him to decrease rather than to grow as he proceeded. Indeed he soon found that he could go forward at all only by remembering Mr. Wisdom's Absolute incessantly. It was necessary by repeated efforts of the will to turn thither, consciously to draw from that endless reservoir the little share of vitality that he needed for the next narrow place. He knew now that he was praying, but he thought that he had drawn the fangs of that knowledge. In a sense, he said, Spirit is not I. I am it, but I am not the whole of it. When I turn back to that part of it which is not I—that far greater part which my soul does not exhaust—surely that part is to me an Other. It must become, for my imagination, not really "I" but "Thou." A metaphor—perhaps more than a metaphor. Of course there is no need at all to confuse it with the *mythical* Landlord. . . . However I think of it, I think of it inadequately.

Then a new thing happened to John, and he began to sing: and this is as much of his song as I remember from my dream

> He whom I bow to only knows to whom I bow
> When I attempt the ineffable name, murmuring *Thou*;
> And dream of Pheidian fancies and embrace in heart
> Meanings, I know, that cannot be the thing thou art.
> All prayers always, taken at their word, blaspheme,
> Invoking with frail imageries a folk-lore dream;
> And all men are idolaters, crying unheard
> To senseless idols, if thou take them at their word,
> And all men in their praying, self-deceived, address

One that is not (so saith that old rebuke) unless
Thou, of mere grace, appropriate, and to thee divert
Men's arrows, all at hazard aimed, beyond desert.
Take not, oh Lord, our literal sense, but in thy great,
Unbroken speech our halting metaphor translate.

When he came to think over the words that had gone out
of him he began once more to be afraid of them. Day was
declining and in the narrow chasm it was already almost
dark.

The Invisible Presence

WHAT PUT A STOP TO ALL THIS was a sudden fright. Shasta
discovered that someone or somebody was walking beside
him. It was pitch dark and he could see nothing. And the
Thing (or Person) was going so quietly that he could hardly
hear any footfalls. What he could hear was breathing. His
invisible companion seemed to breathe on a very large
scale, and Shasta got the impression that it was a very large
creature. And he had come to notice this breathing so gradually that he had really no idea how long it had been there.
It was a horrible shock.

It darted into his mind that he had heard long ago that
there were giants in these Northern countries. He bit his lip
in terror. But now that he really had something to cry
about, he stopped crying.

The Thing (unless it was a Person) went on beside him so
very quietly that Shasta began to hope he had only imagined it. But just as he was becoming quite sure of it, there
suddenly came a deep, rich sigh out of the darkness beside
him. That couldn't be imagination! Anyway, he had felt the
hot breath of that sigh on his chily left hand.

If the horse had been any good—or if he had known how to get any good out of the horse—he would have risked everything on a break away and a wild gallop. But he knew he couldn't make that horse gallop. So he went on at a walking pace and the unseen companion walked and breathed beside him. At last he could bear it no longer.

"Who are you?" he said, scarcely above a whisper.

"One who has waited long for you to speak," said the Thing. Its voice was not loud, but very large and deep.

"Are you—are you a giant?" asked Shasta.

"You might call me a giant," said the Large Voice. "But I am not like the creatures you call giants."

"I can't see you at all," said Shasta, after staring very hard. Then (for an even more terrible idea had come into his head) he said, almost in a scream, "You're not—not something *dead*, are you? Oh please—please do go away. What harm have I ever done you? Oh, I am the unluckiest person in the whole world."

Once more he felt the warm breath of the Thing on his hand and face. "There," it said, "that is not the breath of a ghost. Tell me your sorrows."

Shasta was a little reassured by the breath: so he told how he had never known his real father or mother and had been brought up sternly by the fisherman. And then he told the story of his escape and how they were chased by lions and forced to swim for their lives; and of all their dangers in Tashbaan and about his night among the Tombs and how the beasts howled at him out of the desert. And he told about the heat and thirst of their desert journey and how they were almost at their goal when another lion chased them and wounded Aravis. And also, how very long it was since he had had anything to eat.

"I do not call you unfortunate," said the Large Voice.

"Don't you think it was bad luck to meet so many lions?" said Shasta.

"There was only one lion," said the Voice.

"What on earth do you mean? I've just told you there were at least two the first night, and——"

"There was only one: but he was swift of foot."

"How do you know?"

"I was the lion." And as Shasta gaped with open mouth and said nothing, the Voice continued. "I was the lion who forced you to join with Aravis. I was the cat who comforted you among the houses of the dead. I was the lion who drove the jackals from you while you slept. I was the lion who gave the Horses the new strength of fear for the last mile so that you should reach King Lune in time. And I was the lion you do not remember who pushed the boat in which you lay, a child near death, so that it came to shore where a man sat, wakeful at midnight, to receive you."

"Then it was you who wounded Aravis?"

"It was I."

"But what for?"

"Child," said the Voice, "I am telling you your story, not hers. I tell no-one any story but his own."

"Who *are* you?" asked Shasta.

"Myself," said the Voice, very deep and low so that the earth shook: and again "Myself," loud and clear and gay: and then the third time "Myself," whispered so softly you could hardly hear it, and yet it seemed to come from all round you as if the leaves rustled with it.

Shasta was no longer afraid that the Voice belonged to something that would eat him, nor that it was the voice of a ghost. But a new and different sort of trembling came over him. Yet he felt glad too.

The mist was turning from black to grey and from grey to white. This must have begun to happen some time ago, but while he had been talking to the Thing he had not been noticing anything else. Now, the whiteness around him became a shining whiteness; his eyes began to blink. Somewhere ahead he could hear birds singing. He knew the night was over at last. He could see the mane and ears and head of his horse quite easily now. A golden light fell on them from the left. He thought it was the sun.

He turned and saw, pacing beside him, taller than the horse, a Lion. The horse did not seem to be afraid of it or else could not see it. It was from the lion that the light came. No-one ever saw anything more terrible or beautiful.

Luckily Shasta had lived all his life too far south in Calormen to have heard the tales that were whispered in Tashbaan about a dreadful Narnian demon that appeared in the form of a lion. And of course he knew none of the true stories about Aslan, the great Lion, the son of the Emperor-over-sea, the King above all High Kings in Narnia. But after one glance at the Lion's face he slipped out of the saddle and fell at its feet. He couldn't say anything but then he didn't want to say anything, and he knew he needn't say anything.

The High King above all kings stooped towards him. Its mane, and some strange and solemn perfume that hung about the mane, was all round him. It touched his forehead with its tongue. He lifted his face and their eyes met. Then instantly the pale brightness of the mist and the fiery brightness of the Lion rolled themselves together into a swirling glory and gathered themselves up and disappeared. He was alone with the horse on a grassy hillside under a blue sky. And there were birds singing.

A Moment of Vision

IT WAS ALREADY TWILIGHT and there was much mist in the valley. The pools of the river as I went down to it to drink (for I was thirsty as well as cold) seemed to be dark holes in the greyness. And I got my drink, ice-cold, and I thought it steadied my mind. But would a river flowing in the gods' secret valley do that, or the clean contrary? This is another of the things to be guessed. For when I lifted my head and looked once more into the mist across the water, I saw that which brought my heart into my throat. There stood the palace, grey—as all things were grey in that hour and place—but solid and motionless, wall within wall, pillar and arch and architrave, acres of it, a labyrinthine beauty. As she had said, it was like no house ever seen in our land or age. Pinnacles and buttresses leaped up—no memories of mine, you would think, could help me to imagine them— unbelievably tall and slender, pointed and prickly as if stone were shooting out into branch and flower. No light showed from any window. It was a house asleep. And somewhere within it, asleep also, someone or something— how holy, or horrible, or beautiful or strange?—with Psyche in its arms. And I, what had I done and said? what would it do to me for my blasphemies and unbelievings? I never doubted that I must now cross the river, or try to cross it, even if it should drown me. I must lie on the steps at the great gate of that house and make my petition. I must ask forgiveness of Psyche as well as of the god. I had dared to scold her (dared, what was worse, to try to comfort her as a child) but all the time she was far above me; herself now hardly mortal. . . . if what I saw was real. I was in great fear. Perhaps it was not real. I looked and looked to see if it would not fade or change. Then as I rose (for all this time I was still kneeling where I had drunk), almost before I stood on my feet, the whole thing was vanished. There was a tiny space of time in which I thought I could see how some swirlings of the mist had looked, for the moment, like towers and walls. But very soon, no likeness at all. I was staring simply into fog, and my eyes smarting with it.

And now, you who read, give judgement. That moment when I either saw or thought I saw the House—does it tell against the gods or against me? Would they (if they answered) make it a part of their defence? say it was a sign, a hint, beckoning me to answer the riddle one way rather than the other? I'll not grant them that. What is the use of a sign which is itself only another riddle? It might—I'll allow so much—it might have been a true seeing; the cloud over my mortal eyes may have been lifted for a moment. It might not; what would be easier than for one distraught and not, maybe, so fully waking as she seemed, gazing at a mist, in a half-light, to fancy what had filled her thoughts for so many hours?

The Nativity

THE TURN OF THE TIDE

Breathless was the air over Bethlehem. Black and bare
    Were the fields; hard as granite the clods;
Hedges stiff with ice; the sedge in the vice
    Of the pool, like pointed iron rods.
And the deathly stillness spread from Bethlehem. It was
    shed
    Wider each moment on the land;
Through rampart and wall into camp and into hall
    Stole the hush; all tongues were at a stand.
At the Procurator's feast the jocular freedman ceased
    His story, and gaped. All were glum.
Travellers at their beer in a tavern turned to hear
    The landlord; their oracle was dumb.
But the silence flowed forth to the islands and the North
    And smoothed the unquiet river bars
And levelled out the waves from their revelling and paved
    The sea with cold reflected stars.
Where the Caesar on Palatine sat at ease to sign,
    Without anger, signatures of death,
There stole into his room and on his soul a gloom,
    And his pen faltered, and his breath.
Then to Carthage and the Gauls, past Parthia and the Falls
    Of Nile and Mount Amara it crept;
The romp and war of beast in swamp and jungle ceased,
    The forest grew still as though it slept.
So it ran about the girth of the planet. From the Earth
    A signal, a warning, went out
And away behind the air. Her neighbours were aware
    Of change. They were troubled with a doubt.

Salamanders in the Sun that brandish as they run
    Tails like the Americas in size
Were stunned by it and dazed; wondering, they gazed
    Up at Earth, misgiving in their eyes.
In Houses and Signs Ousiarchs divine
    Grew pale and questioned what it meant;
Great Galactal lords stood back to back with swords
    Half-drawn, awaiting the event,
And a whisper among them passed, 'Is this perhaps the last
    Of our story and the glories of our crown?
—The entropy worked out?—The central redoubt
    Abandoned? The world-spring running down?'
Then they could speak no more. Weakness overbore
    Even them. They were as flies in a web,
In their lethargy stone-dumb. The death had almost come;
    The tide lay motionless at ebb.

Like a stab at that moment, over Crab and Bowman,
    Over Maiden and Lion, came the shock
Of returning life, the start and burning pang at heart,
    Setting Galaxies to tingle and rock;
And the Lords dared to breathe, and swords were sheathed
    And a rustling, a relaxing began,
With a rumour and noise of the resuming of joys,
    On the nerves of the universe it ran.
Then pulsing into space with delicate, dulcet pace
    Came a music, infinitely small
And clear. But it swelled and drew nearer and held
    All worlds in the sharpness of its call.
And now divinely deep, and louder, with the sweep
    And quiver of inebriating sound,
The vibrant dithyramb shook Libra and the Ram,
    The brains of Aquarius spun round;
Such a note as neither Throne nor Potentate had known
    Since the Word first founded the abyss,
But this time it was changed in a mystery, estranged,

A paradox, an ambiguous bliss.
Heaven danced to it and burned. Such answer was returned
     To the hush, the *Favete*, the fear
That Earth had sent out; revel, mirth and shout
     Descended to her, sphere below sphere.
Saturn laughed and lost his latter age's frost,
     His beard, Niagara-like, unfroze;
Monsters in the Sun rejoiced; the Inconstant One,
     The unwedded Moon, forgot her woes.
A shiver of re-birth and deliverance on the Earth
     Went gliding. Her bonds were released.
Into broken light a breeze rippled and woke the seas,
     In the forest it startled every beast.
Capripods fell to dance from Taproban to France,
     Leprechauns from Down to Labrador,
In his green Asian dell the Phoenix from his shell
     Burst forth and was the Phoenix once more.

So death lay in arrest. But at Bethlehem the bless'd
     Nothing greater could be heard
Than a dry wind in the thorn, the cry of the One new-born,
     And cattle in stall as they stirred.

A Numinous Name

"THEY SAY ASLAN IS ON THE MOVE—perhaps has already landed."

And now a very curious thing happened. None of the children knew who Aslan was any more than you do; but the moment the Beaver had spoken these words everyone felt quite different. Perhaps it has sometimes happened to you in a dream that someone says something which you don't understand but in the dream it feels as if it had some enormous meaning—either a terrifying one which turns the whole dream into a nightmare or else a lovely meaning too lovely to put into words, which makes the dream so beautiful that you remember it all your life and are always wishing you could get into that dream again. It was like that now. At the name of Aslan each one of the children felt something jump in his inside. Edmund felt a sensation of mysterious horror. Peter felt suddenly brave and adventurous. Susan felt as if some delicious smell or some delightful strain of music had just floated by her. And Lucy got the feeling you have when you wake up in the morning and realise that it is the beginning of the holidays or the beginning of summer.

A Numinous Place

NOW WE WERE AT THE BOTTOM, and so warm that I had half a mind to dip my hands and face in the swift, amber water of the stream which still divided us from the main of the valley. I had already lifted my hand to put aside my veil when I heard two voices cry out—one, Bardia's. I looked. A quivering shock of feeling that has no name (but is nearest terror) stabbed through me from head to foot. There, not six feet away, on the far side of the river, stood Psyche.

What I babbled, between tears and laughter, in the first wildness of my joy (the water still between us) I don't know. I was recalled by Bardia's voice.

"Careful, Lady. It may be her wraith. It may—ai! ai!—it is the bride of the god. It is a goddess." He was deadly white and bending down to throw earth on his forehead.

You could not blame him. She was so brightface, as we say in Greek. But I felt no holy fear. What?—I to fear the very Psyche whom I had carried in my arms and taught to speak and to walk? She was tanned by sun and wind, and clothed in rags, but laughing—her eyes like two stars, her limbs smooth and rounded, and (but for the rags) no sign of beggary or hardship about her.

"Welcome, welcome, welcome," she was saying. "Oh, Maia, I have longed for this. It was my only longing. I knew you would come. Oh, how happy I am! And good Bardia, too. It was he that brought you? Of course; I might have guessed it. Come, Orual, you must cross the stream. I'll show you where it's easiest. But, Bardia—I can't bid you across. Dear Bardia, it's not—"

"No, no, Blessed Istra," said Bardia (and I thought he was very relieved). "I'm only a soldier." Then, in a lower voice, to me, "Will you go, Lady? This is a very dreadful place. Perhaps—"

"Go?" said I. "I'd go if the river flowed with fire instead of water."

"Of course," said he. "It's not with you as with us. You have gods' blood in you. I'll stay here with the horse. We're out of the wind and there's good grass for him here."

I was already on the edge of the river.

"A little further up, Orual," Psyche was saying. "Here's the best ford. Go straight ahead off that big stone. Gently! make your footing sure. No, not to your left. It's very deep in places. This way. Now, one step more. Reach out for my hand."

I suppose the long bed-ridden and in-doors time of my sickness had softened me. Anyhow, the coldness of that water shocked all the breath out of me; and the current was so strong that, but for Psyche's hand, I think it would have knocked me down and rolled me under. I even thought, momentarily amid a thousand other things, "How strong she grows. She'll be a stronger woman than ever I was. She'll have that as well as her beauty."

The next was all a confusion—trying to talk, to cry, to kiss, to get my breath back, all together. But she led me a few paces beyond the river and made me sit in the warm heather, and sat beside me, our four hands joined in my lap, just as it had been that night in her prison.

"Why, Sister," she said merrily, "you have found my threshold cold and steep! You are breathless. But I'll refresh you."

She jumped up, went a little way off, and came back, carrying something; the little cool, dark berries of the Mountain, in a green leaf. "Eat," she said. "Is it not food fit for the gods?"

"Nothing sweeter," said I. And indeed I was both hungry and thirsty enough by now, for it was noon or later. "But oh, Psyche, tell me how—"

"Wait!" said she. "After the banquet, the wine." Close beside us a little silvery trickle came out from among stones mossed cushion-soft. She held her two hands under it till they were filled and raised them to my lips.

"Have you ever tasted a nobler wine?" she said. "Or in a fairer cup?"

The Plunge of Faith

"WHAT MUST I DO?" said John.

"You must take off your rags," said she, "as your friend has done already, and then you must dive into this water."

"Alas," said he, "I have never learned to dive."

"There is nothing to learn," said she. "The art of diving is not to do anything new but simply to cease doing something. You have only to let yourself go."

"It is only necessary," said Vertue, with a smile, "to abandon all efforts at self-preservation."

"I think," said John, "that if it is all one, I would rather jump."

"It is not all one," said Mother Kirk. "If you jump, you will be trying to save yourself and you may be hurt. As well, you would not go deep enough. You must dive so that you can go right down to the bottom of the pool: for you are not to come up again on this side. There is a tunnel in the cliff, far beneath the surface of the water, and it is through that that you must pass so that you may come up on the far side."

"I see," thought John to himself, "that they have brought me here to kill me," but he began, nevertheless, to take off his clothes. They were little loss to him, for they hung in shreds, plastered with blood and with the grime of every shire from Puritania to the canyon: but they were so stuck to him that they came away with pain and a little skin came with them. When he was naked Mother Kirk bade him come to the edge of the pool, where Vertue was already standing. It was a long way down to the water, and the reflected moon seemed to look up at him from the depth of a mine. He had had some thought of throwing himself in, with a run, the very instant he reached the edge, before he had time to be afraid. And the making of that resolution had seemed to be itself the bitterness of death, so that he half believed the worst must be over and that he would find himself in the water before he knew. But lo! he was still standing on the edge, still on this side. Then a stranger thing came to pass. From the great concourse of spectators, shadowy people came stealing out to his side, touching his arm and whispering to him: and every one of them appeared to be the wraith of some old acquaintance.

First came the wraith of old Enlightenment and said, "There's still time. Get away and come back to me and all this will vanish like a nightmare."

Then came the wraith of Media Halfways and said, "Can you really risk losing me for ever? I know you do not desire me at this moment. But for ever? Think. Don't burn your boats."

And the wraith of old Halfways said, "After all—has this anything to do with the Island as you used to imagine it? Come back and hear my songs instead. You *know* them."

The wraith of young Halfways said, "Aren't you ashamed? Be a man. Move with the times and don't throw your life away for an old wives' tale."

The wraith of Sigmund said, "You know what this is, I suppose. Religious melancholia. Stop while there is time. If you dive, you dive into insanity."

The wraith of Sensible said, "Safety first. A touch of rational piety adds something to life: but this salvationist business . . . well! Who knows where it will end? Never accept unlimited liabilities."

The wraith of Humanist said, "Mere atavism. You are diving to escape your real duties. All this emotionalism, after the first plunge, is so much *easier* than virtue in the classical sense."

The wraith of Broad said, "My dear boy, you are losing your head. These sudden conversions and violent struggles don't achieve anything. We have had to discard so much that our ancestors thought necessary. It is all far easier, far more gracious and beautiful than they supposed."

But at that moment the voice of Vertue broke in:

"Come on, John," he said, "the longer we look at it the less we shall like it," And with that he took a header into the pool and they saw him no more. And how John managed it or what he felt I did not know, but he also rubbed his hands, shut his eyes, despaired, and let himself go. It was not a good dive, but, at least, he reached the water head first.

The Voice of a God

SO AT LAST, fainting with weariness, out beyond the city and down to the river; I myself had made it deep. The old Shennit, as she was before my works, would not, save in spate, have drowned even a crone.

I had to go a little way along the river to a place where I knew that the bank was high, so that I could fling myself down; for I doubted my courage to wade in and feel death first up to my knee, and then to my belly, and then to my neck, and still to go on. When I came to the high bank I took my girdle and tied my ankles together with it lest even in my old age I might save my life, or lengthen my death, by swimming. Then I straightened myself, panting from the labour, and stood footfast like a prisoner.

I hopped—what blending of misery and buffoonery it would have looked if I could have seen it!—hopped with my strapped feet a little nearer to the edge.

A voice came from beyond the river: "Do not do it."

Instantly—I had been freezing cold till now—a wave of fire passed over me, even down to my numb feet. It was the voice of a god. Who should know better than I? A god's voice had once shattered my whole life. They are not to be mistaken. It may well be that by trickery of priests men have sometimes taken a mortal's voice for a god's. But it will not work the other way. No one who hears a god's voice takes it for a mortal's.

"Lord, who are you?" said I.

"Do not do it," said the god. "You cannot escape Ungit by going to the deadlands, for she is there also. Die before you die. There is no chance after."

"Lord, I am Ungit."

But there was no answer. And that is another thing about

the voices of the gods; when once they have ceased, though it is only a heart-beat ago and the bright hard syllables, the heavy bars or mighty obelisks of sound, are still master in your ears, it is as if they had ceased a thousand years before, and to expect further utterance is like asking for an apple from a tree that fruited the day the world was made.

The voice of the god had not changed in all those years, but I had. There was no rebel in me now. I must not drown and doubtless should not be able to.

I crawled home, troubling the quiet city once more with my dark witch-shape and my tapping stick. And when I laid my head on my pillow it seemed but a moment before my women came to wake me, whether because the whole journey had been a dream or because my weariness (which would be no wonder) had thrown me into a very fast sleep.

Magic

AT THE BEGINNING the grand mystery for the Company had been why the enemy wanted Bragdon Wood. The land was unsuitable and could be made fit to bear a building on the scale they proposed only by the costliest preliminary work; and Edgestow itself was not an obviously convenient place. By intense study in collaboration with Dr. Dimble, and despite the continued scepticism of MacPhee, the Director had at last come to a certain conclusion. Dimble and he and the Dennistons shared between them a knowledge of Arthurian Britain which orthodox scholarship will probably not reach for some centuries. They knew that Edgestow lay in what had been the very heart of ancient Logres, that the village of Cure Hardy preserved the name of Ozana le Coeur Hardi, and that a historical Merlin had once worked in what was now Bragdon Wood.

What exactly he had done there they did not know; but they had all, by various routes, come too far either to consider his art mere legend and imposture, or to equate it exactly with what the Renaissance called Magic. Dimble even maintained that a good critic, by his sensibility alone, could detect the difference between the traces which the two things had left on literature. "What common measure is there," he would ask, "between ceremonial occultists like Faustus and Prospero and Archimago with their midnight studies, their forbidden books, their attendant fiends or elementals, and a figure like Merlin who seems to produce his results simply by being Merlin?" And Ransom agreed. He thought that Merlin's art was the last survival of something older and different—something brought to Western Europe after the fall of Numinor and going back to an era in which the general relations of mind and matter on this planet had been other than those we know. It had probably differed from Renaissance Magic profoundly. It had possibly (though this was doubtful) been less guilty: it had certainly been more effective. For Paracelsus and Agrippa and the rest had achieved little or nothing: Bacon himself—no enemy to magic except on this account—reported that the magicians "attained not to greatness and certainty of works." The whole Renaissance outburst of forbidden arts had, it seemed, been a method of losing one's soul on singularly unfavourable terms. But the older Art had been a different proposition.

The Occult*

15

And all his talk was tales of magic words
And of the nations in the clouds above,
Astral and aerish tribes who fish for birds
With angles. And by history he could prove
How chosen spirits from earth had won their love,
As Arthur, or Usheen: and to their isle
Went Helen for the sake of a Greek smile.

16

And ever in his talk he mustered well
His texts and strewed old authors round the way,
"Thus Wierus writes," and "Thus the Hermetics tell,"
"This was Agrippa's view," and "Others say
With Cardan," till he had stolen quite away
Dymer's dull wits and softly drawn apart
The ivory gates of hope that change the heart.

17

Dymer was talking now. Now Dymer told
Of his own love and losing, drowsily.
The Master leaned towards him, "Was it cold,
This spirit, to the touch?"—"No, Sir, not she,"
Said Dymer. And his host: "Why this must be
Aethereal, not aerial! O my soul,
Be still . . . but wait. Tell on, Sir, tell the whole."

18

Then Dymer told him of the beldam too,
The old, old, matriarchal dreadfulness.

*From *Dymer*.

Over the Master's face a shadow drew,
He shifted in his chair and "Yes" and "Yes,"
He murmured twice. "I never looked for less!
Always the same . . . that frightful woman shape
Besets the dream-way and the soul's escape."

19

But now when Dymer made to talk of Bran,
A huge indifference fell upon his host,
Patient and wandering-eyed. Then he began,
"Forgive me. You are young. What helps us most
Is to find out again that heavenly ghost
Who loves you. For she was a ghost, and you
In that place where you met were ghostly too.

20

"Listen! for I can launch you on the stream
Will roll you to the shores of her own land . . .
I could be sworn you never learned to dream,
But every night you take with careless hand
What chance may bring? I'll teach you to command
The comings and the goings of your spirit
Through all that borderland which dreams inherit.

21

"You shall have hauntings suddenly. And often,
When you forget, when least you think of her
(For so you shall forget), a light will soften
Over the evening woods. And in the stir
Of morning dreams (oh, I will teach you, Sir)
There'll come a sound of wings. Or you shall be
Waked in the midnight murmuring, 'It was she.' "

22

"No, no," said Dymer, "not that way. I seem
To have slept for twenty years. Now—while I shake

Out of my eyes that dust of burdening dream,
Now when the long clouds tremble ripe to break
And the far hills appear, when first I wake,
Still blinking, struggling towards the world of men,
And longing—would you turn me back again?

23

"Dreams? I have had my dream too long. I thought
The sun rose for my sake. I ran down blind
And dancing to the abyss. Oh, Sir, I brought
Boy-laughter for a gift to gods who find
The martyr's soul too soft. But that's behind.
I'm waking now. They broke me. All ends thus
Always—and we're for them, not they for us.

24

"And she—she was no dream. It would be waste
To seek her there, the living in that den
Of lies." The Master smiled. "You are in haste!
For broken dreams the cure is, Dream again
And deeper. If the waking world, and men,
And nature marred your dream—so much the worse
For a crude world beneath its primal curse."

25

—"Ah, but you do not know! Can dreams do this,
Pluck out blood-guiltiness upon the shore
Of memory—and undo what's done amiss,
And bid the thing that has been be no more?"
—"Sir, it is only dreams unlock that door,"
He answered with a shrug. "What would you have?
In dreams the thrice-proved coward can feel brave.

26

"In dreams the fool is free from scorning voices.
Grey-headed whores are virgin there again.

Out of the past dream brings long-buried choices,
All in a moment snaps the tenfold chain
That life took years in forging. There the stain
Of oldest sins—how do the good works go?—
Though they were scarlet, shall be white as snow."

Martyrdom *

The Leader's ruffians gather with great strokes
About the Bishop, with lead pipe and sticks,
As foresters about a tree with the axe,
With belts and bludgeons and with jibes and jokes.
His breath comes grunting under heavy shocks,
He pants so loud, they think that he still talks,
And rail upon him crying Plague and Pox!
Ever a bone breaks or a sinew cracks.
They beat upon his stomach till its wall breaks.   Aoi!

In his imagination he seems to hang
Upon a cross and be tormented long,
Not nailed but gripping with his fingers strong.
With the toil thereof all his muscles are wrung,
Great pains he bears in shoulder, arm and lung.
He fears lest they should jolt the cross and fling
His body off from where he has to hang.   Aoi!

Ever he calls to Christ to be forgiven
And to come soon into the happy haven.
Horrible dance before his eyes is woven
Of darkened shapes on a red tempest driven.
Unwearyingly the great strokes are given.
He falls. His sides and all his ribs are riven,
His guts are scattered and his skull is cloven,
The man is dead. God has his soul to heaven.   Aoi!

*From *The Queen of Drum.*

Masculine and Feminine

THE DIRECTOR LAUGHED; just that loud, assured, bachelor laughter which had often infuriated her on other lips.

"Yes," he said. "But don't think I'm talking of Freudian repressions. He knew only half the facts. It isn't a question of inhibitions—inculcated shame—against natural desire. I'm afraid there's no niche in the world for people that won't be either Pagan or Christian. Just imagine a man who was too dainty to eat with his fingers and yet wouldn't use forks!"

His laughter rather than his words had reddened Jane's cheeks, and she was staring at him open-mouthed. Assuredly, the Director was not in the least like Mother Dimble; but an odious realisation that he was, in this matter, on Mother Dimble's side—that he also, though he did not belong to that hot-coloured, archaic world, stood somehow in good diplomatic relations with it, from which she was excluded—had struck her like a blow. Some old female dream of finding a man who "really understood" was being insulted. She took it for granted, half-unconsciously, that the Director was the most virginal of his sex; but she had not realised that this would leave his masculinity still on the other side of the stream from herself and even steeper, more emphatic, than that of common men. Some knowledge of a world beyond Nature she had already gained from living in his house, and more from fear of death that night in the dingle. But she had been conceiving this world as "spiritual" in the negative sense—as some neutral, or democratic, vacuum where differences disappeared, where sex and sense were not transcended but simply taken away. Now the suspicion dawned upon her that there might be differences and contrasts all the way up, richer, sharper, even fiercer, at every rung of the ascent. How if this invasion of her own being in marriage from which she had recoiled, often in the very teeth of instinct, were not, as she had supposed, merely a relic of animal life or patriarchal barbarism, but rather the lowest, the first, and the easiest form of some shocking contact with reality which would have to be repeated—but in ever larger and more disturbing modes—on the highest levels of all?

"Yes," said the Director. "There is no escape. If it were a virginal rejection of the male, He would allow it. Such souls can bypass the male and go on to meet something far more masculine, higher up, to which they must make a yet deeper surrender. But your trouble has been what old poets called *Daungier*. We call it Pride. You are offended by the masculine itself: the loud, irruptive, possessive thing—the gold lion, the bearded bull—which breaks through hedges and scatters the little kingdom of your primness as the dwarfs scattered the carefully made bed. The male you could have escaped, for it exists only on the biological level. But the masculine none of us can escape. What is above and beyond all things is so masculine that we are all feminine in relation to it. You had better agree with your adversary quickly."

"You mean I shall have to become a Christian?" said Jane.

"It looks like it," said the Director.

Human Sacrifice

"BY THE KING'S PERMISSION," said the Fox, "the shepherd's tale is very questionable. If the man had a torch, of necessity the lion would have a big black shadow behind it. The man was scared and new waked from sleep. He took a shadow for a monster."

"That is the wisdom of the Greeks," said the Priest. "But Glome does not take counsel with slaves, not even if they are kings' favourites. And if the Brute was a shadow, King, what then? Many say it *is* a shadow. But if that shadow begins coming down into the city, look to yourself. You are of divine blood and doubtless fear nothing. But the people will fear. Their fear will be so great that not even I will be able to hold them. They will burn your palace about your ears. They will bar you in before they burn it. You would be wiser to make the Great Offering."

"How is it made?" said the King. "It has never happened in my time."

"It is not done in the house of Ungit," said the Priest. "The victim must be given to the Brute. For the Brute is, in a mystery, Ungit herself or Ungit's son, the god of the Mountain; or both. The victim is led up the mountain to the Holy Tree, and bound to the Tree and left. Then the Brute comes. That is why you angered Ungit just now, King, when you spoke of offering a thief. In the Great Offering, the victim must be perfect. For, in holy language, a man so offered is said to be Ungit's husband, and a woman is said to be the bride of Ungit's son. And both are called the Brute's Supper. And when the Brute is Ungit it lies with the man, and when it is her son it lies with the woman. And either way there is a devouring . . . many different things are said . . . many sacred stories . . . many great mysteries. Some say the loving and the devouring are all the same thing. For in sacred language we say that a woman who lies with a man devours the man. That is why you are so wide of the mark, King, when you think a thief, or an old worn-out slave, or a coward taken in battle, would do for the Great Offering. The best in the land is not too good for this office."

The Police Function

IT WOULD BE MISLEADING to say that he liked her. She had indeed excited in him all the distaste which a young man feels at the proximity of something rankly, even insolently sexed, and at the same time wholly unattractive. And something in her cold eye had told him that she was well aware of this reaction and found it amusing. She had told him a good many smoking-room stories. Often before now Mark had shuddered at the clumsy efforts of the emancipated female to indulge in this kind of humour, but his shudders had always been consoled by a sense of superiority. This time he had the feeling that he was the butt; this woman was exasperating male prudery for her diversion. Later on, she drifted into police reminiscences. In spite of some initial scepticism, Mark was gradually horrified by her assumption that about thirty per cent of our murder trials ended by the hanging of an innocent man. There were details, too, about the execution shed which had not occurred to him before.

All this was disagreeable. But it was made up for by the deliciously esoteric character of the conversation. Several times that day he had been made to feel himself an outsider; that feeling completely disappeared while Miss Hardcastle was talking to him. He had the sense of getting *in*. Miss Hardcastle had apparently lived an exciting life. She had been, at different times, a suffragette, a pacifist, and a British Fascist. She had been manhandled by the police and imprisoned. On the other hand, she had met Prime Ministers, Dictators, and famous film stars; all her history was secret history. She knew from both ends what a police force could do and what it could not, and there were in her opinion very few things it could not do. "Specially now," she said. "Here in the Institute, we're backing the crusade against Red Tape."

Mark gathered that, for the Fairy, the police side of the Institute was the really important side. It existed to relieve the ordinary executive of what might be called all sanitary cases—a category which ranged from vaccination to charges of unnatural vice—from which, as she pointed out, it was only a step to bringing in all cases of blackmail. As regards crime in general, they had already popularised in the press the idea that the Institute should be allowed to experiment pretty largely in the hope of discovering how far humane, remedial treatment could be substituted for the old notion of "retributive" or "vindictive" punishment. That was where a lot of legal Red Tape stood in their way. "But there are only two papers we don't control," said the Fairy. "And we'll smash them. You've got to get the ordinary man into the state in which he says 'Sadism' automatically when he hears the word Punishment." And then one would have *carte blanche*. Mark did not immediately follow this. But the Fairy pointed out that what had hampered every English police force up to date was precisely the idea of deserved punishment. For desert was always finite: you could do so much to the criminal and no more. Remedial treatment, on the other hand, need have no fixed limit; it could go on till it had effected a cure, and those who were carrying it out would decide when *that* was. And if cure were humane and desirable, how much more prevention? Soon anyone who had ever been in the hands of the police at all would come under the control of the N.I.C.E.; in the end, every citizen. "And that's where you and I come in, Sonny," added the Fairy, tapping Mark's chest with her forefinger. "There's no distinction in the long run between police work and sociology. You and I've got to work hand in hand."

Spiritual Eyes

"PSYCHE," said I, leaping up, "I can't bear this any longer. You have told me so many wonders. If this is all true, I've been wrong all my life. Everything has to be begun over again. Psyche, it is true? You're not playing a game with me? Show me. Show me your palace."

"Of course I will," she said, rising. "Let us go in. And don't be afraid whatever you see or hear."

"Is it far?" said I.

She gave me a quick, astonished look. "Far to where?" she said.

"To the palace, to this god's House."

You have seen a lost child in a crowd run up to a woman whom it takes for its mother, and how the woman turns round and shows the face of a stranger, and then the look in the child's eyes, silent a moment before it begins to cry. Psyche's face was like that; checked, blank; happiest assurance suddenly dashed all to pieces.

"Orual," she said, beginning to tremble, "what do you mean?"

I too became frightened, though I had yet no notion of the truth. "Mean?" said I. "Where is the palace? How far have we to go to reach it?"

She gave one loud cry. Then, with white face, staring hard into my eyes, she said, "But *this* is it, Orual! It is here! You are standing on the stairs of the great gate."

Spiritual Combat with Fists

HE FELL BACK on a different line of defence. How *could* he fight the immortal enemy? Even if he were a fighting man— instead of a sedentary scholar with weak eyes and a bad- dish wound from the last war—what use was there in fight- ing it? It couldn't be killed, could it? But the answer was almost immediately plain. Weston's body could be de- stroyed; and presumably that body was the Enemy's only foothold in Perelandra. By that body, when that body still obeyed a human will, it had entered the new world: ex- pelled from it, it would doubtless have no other habitation. It had entered that body at Weston's own invitation, and without such invitation could enter no other. Ransom re- membered that the unclean spirits, in the Bible, had a hor- ror of being cast out into the "deep." And thinking of these things he perceived at last, with a sinking of heart, that if physical action were indeed demanded of him, it was an action, by ordinary standards, neither impossible nor hope- less. On the physical plane it was one middle-aged, seden- tary body against another, and both unarmed save for fists and teeth and nails. At the thought of these details, terror and disgust overcame him. To kill the thing with such weapons (he remembered his killing of the frog) would be a nightmare; to be killed—who knew how slowly?—was more than he could face. That he would be killed he felt certain. "When," he asked, "did I ever win a fight in all my life?"

He was no longer making efforts to resist the conviction of what he must do. He had exhausted all his efforts. The answer was plain beyond all subterfuge. The Voice out of the night spoke it to him in such unanswerable fashion that, though there was no noise, he almost felt it must wake the woman who slept close by. He was faced with the impossible. This he must do: this he could not do. In vain he reminded himself of the things that unbelieving boys might at this moment be doing on Earth for a lesser cause. His will was in that valley where the appeal to shame becomes useless—nay, makes the valley darker and deeper. He believed he could face the Unman with firearms: even that he could stand up unarmed and face certain death if the creature had retained Weston's revolver. But to come to grips with it, to go voluntarily into those dead yet living arms, to grapple with it, naked chest to naked chest. . . . Terrible follies came into his mind. He would fail to obey the Voice, but it would be all right because he would repent later on, when he was back on Earth. He would lose his nerve as St. Peter had done, and be, like St. Peter, forgiven. Intellectually, of course, he knew the answer to these temptations perfectly well; but he was at one of those moments when all the utterances of intellect sound like twicetold tales. Then some cross-wind of the mind changed his mood. Perhaps he would fight and win, perhaps not even be badly mauled. But no faintest hint of a guarantee in that direction came to him from the darkness. The future was black as the night itself.

"It is not for nothing that you are named Ransom," said the Voice.

A Theological Debate

"It's all true, you know," he said at last.

"What's all true?" said Ransom.

Suddenly Weston turned on him with a snarl of rage. "It's all very well for *you*," he said. "Drowning doesn't hurt and death is bound to come anyway, and all that nonsense. What do *you* know about death? It's all true, I tell you."

"What are you talking about?"

"I've been stuffing myself up with a lot of nonsense all my life," said Weston. "Trying to persuade myself that it matters what happens to the human race . . . trying to believe that anything you can do will make the universe bearable. It's all rot, do you see?"

"And something else is truer!"

"Yes," said Weston, and then was silent for a long time.

"We'd better turn our fishes head on to this," said Ransom presently, his eyes on the seas, "or we'll be driven apart." Weston obeyed without seeming to notice what he did, and for a time the two men were riding very slowly side by side.

"I'll tell you what's truer," said Weston presently.

"What?"

"A little child that creeps upstairs when nobody's looking and very slowly turns the handle to take one peep into the room where its grandmother's dead body is laid out—and then runs away and has bad dreams. An enormous grandmother, you understand."

"What do you mean by saying that's truer?"

"I mean that child knows something about the universe which all science and all religion is trying to hide."

Ransom said nothing.

"Lots of things," said Weston presently. "Children are afraid to go through a churchyard at night, and the grown-ups tell them not to be silly: but the children know better than the grown-ups. People in Central Africa doing beastly things with masks on in the middle of the night—and missionaries and civil servants say it's all superstition. Well, the blacks know more about the universe than the white people. Dirty priests in back streets in Dublin frightening half-witted children to death with stories about it. You'd say they are unenlightened. They're not: except that they think there is a way of escape. There isn't. That is the real universe, always will be. That's what it all *means.*"

"I'm not quite clear——" began Ransom, when Weston interrupted him.

"That's why it's so important to live as long as you can. All the good things are now—a thin little rind of what we call life, put on for show, and then—the *real* universe for ever and ever. To thicken the rind by one centimetre—to live one week, one day, one half-hour longer—that's the only thing that matters. Of course you don't know it: but every man who is waiting to be hanged knows it. You say, 'What difference does a short reprieve make?' What difference!!"

"But nobody need go there," said Ransom.

"I know that's what you believe," said Weston. "But you're wrong. It's only a small parcel of civilised people who think that. Humanity as a whole knows better. It knows—Homer knew—that *all* the dead have sunk down into the inner darkness: under the rind. All witless, all twittering, gibbering, decaying. Bogeymen. Every savage knows that *all* ghosts hate the living who are still enjoying the rind: just as old women hate girls who still have their good looks. It's quite right to be afraid of the ghosts. You're going to be one all the same."

The Fall of Adam and Eve

WHEN THEY WERE SEATED, the old woman [Mother Kirk] told the following story:—

"You must know that once upon a time there were no tenants in this country at all, for the Landlord used to farm it himself. There were only the animals and the Landlord used to look after them, he and his sons and daughters.

Every morning they used to come down from the mountains and milk the cows and lead out the sheep to pasture. And they needed less watching, for all the animals were tamer then; and there were no fences needed, for if a wolf got in among the flocks he would do them no harm. And one day the Landlord was going home from his day's work when he looked round on the country, and the beasts, and saw how the crops were springing, and it came into his head that the whole thing was too good to keep to himself. So he decided to let the country to tenants, and his first tenant was a young married man. But first the Landlord made a farm in the very centre of the land where the soil was the best and the air most wholesome, and that was the very spot where you are sitting now. They were to have the whole land, but that was too much for them to keep under cultivation. The Landlord's idea was that they could work the farm and leave the rest as a park for the time being: but later they could divide the park up into holdings for their children. For you must know that he drew up a very different lease from the kind you have nowadays. It was a lease in perpetuity on his side, for he promised never to turn them out; but on their side, they could leave when they chose, as long as one of their sons was there, to take the farm on, and then they could go up to live with him in the mountains. He thought that would be a good thing because it would broaden the minds of his own mountain children to mix with strangers. And they thought so too. But before he put the tenants in possession there was one thing he had to do. Up to this time the country had been full of a certain fruit which the Landlord had planted for the refreshment of himself and his children, if they were thirsty during the day as they worked down here. It was a very good fruit and up in the mountains they say it is even more plentiful: but it is very strong and only those who are mountain-bred ought to eat it, for only they can digest it properly. Hitherto, while there were only beasts in the land, it had done no harm for these mountain-apples to be growing in every thicket; for you know that an animal will eat nothing but what is good for it. But now that there were to be men in the land, the Landlord was afraid that they might do themselves an injury; yet it was not to be thought of that he should dig up every sapling of that tree and make the country into a desert. So he decided that it was best to be frank with the young people, and when he found a great big mountain-apple tree growing in the very centre of the farm he said, "So much the better. If they are to learn sense, they may as well learn it from the beginning: and if they will not, there's no help for it. For if they did not find mountain-apples on the farm, they would soon find them somewhere else." So he left the apple tree standing, and put the man and his wife into their farm: but before he left them he explained the whole affair to them—as much of it could be explained—and warned them on no account to eat any of the apples. Then he went home. And for a time the young man and his -wife behaved very well, tending the animals and managing their farm, and abstaining from the mountain-apples; and for all I know they might never have done otherwise if the wife had not somehow made a new acquaintance. This new acquaintance was a landowner himself. He had been born in the mountains and was one of our Landlord's own children, but he had quarrelled with his father and set up on his own, and now had built up a very considerable estate in another country. His estate marches, however, with this country: and as he was a great land-grabber he always wanted to take this bit in—and he has very nearly succeeded."

"I've never met any tenants of his," said John.

"Not tenants in chief, my dear," said the old woman. "And so you didn't know them. But you may have met the Clevers, who are tenants of Mr. Mammon: and he is a tenant of the Spirit of the Age: who holds directly of the Enemy."

"I am sure the Clevers would be very surprised," said John, "to hear that they had a Landlord at all. They would think this enemy, as you call him, no less a superstition than *your* Landlord."

"But that is how business is managed," said Mother Kirk. "The little people do not know the big people to whom they belong. The big people do not intend that they should. No important transference of property could be carried out if all the small people at the bottom knew what was really happening. But this is not part of my story. As I was saying, the enemy got to know the farmer's wife: and, however he did it, or whatever he said to her, it wasn't long before he persuaded her that the one thing she needed was a nice mountain-apple. And she took one and ate it. And then— you know how it is with husbands—she made the farmer come round to her mind. And at the moment he put out his hand and plucked the fruit there was an earthquake, and the country cracked open all the way across from North to South: and ever since, instead of the farm, there has been this gorge, which the country people call the Grand Canyon. But in my language its name is *Peccatum Adae*."

The Malacandran Shorter Catechism

THEN HE WAS ASKED how he had come, and made a very poor attempt at describing the space-ship—but again:

"The *séroni* would know."

Had he come alone? No, he had come with two others of his kind—bad men ("bent" men was the nearest *hrossian* equivalent) who tried to kill him, but he had run away from them. The *hrossa* found this very difficult, but all finally agreed that he ought to go to Oyarsa. Oyarsa would protect him. Ransom asked who Oyarsa was. Slowly, and with many misunderstandings, he hammered out the information that Oyarsa (1) lived at Meldilorn; (2) knew everything and ruled everyone; (3) had always been there; and (4) was not a *hross*, nor one of the *séroni*. Then Ransom, following his own idea, asked if Oyarsa had made the world. The *hrossa* almost barked in the fervour of their denial. Did people in Thulcandra not know that Maleldil the Young had made and still ruled the world? Even a child knew that. Where did Maleldil live, Ransom asked.

"With the Old One."

And who was the Old One? Ransom did not understand the answer. He tried again.

"Where was the Old One?"

"He is not that sort," said Hnohra, "that he has to live anywhere," and proceeded to a good deal which Ransom did not follow. But he followed enough to feel once more a certain irritation. Ever since he had discovered the rationality of the *hrossa* he had been haunted by a conscientious scruple as to whether it might not be his duty to undertake their religious instruction; now, as a result of his tentative efforts, he found himself being treated as if *he* were the savage and being given a first sketch of civilized religion—a sort of *hrossian* equivalent of the shorter catechism. It became plain that Maleldil was a spirit without body, parts or passions.

The Ageless Pendragon

ON A SOFA before her, with one foot bandaged as if he had a wound, lay what appeared to be a boy, twenty years old.

On one of the long window sills a tame jackdaw was

walking up and down. The light of the fire with its weak reflection, and the light of the sun with its stronger reflection, contended on the ceiling. But all the light in the room seemed to run towards the gold hair and the gold beard of the wounded man.

Of course he was not a boy—how could she have thought so? The fresh skin on his forehead and cheeks and, above all, on his hands, had suggested the idea. But no boy could have so full a beard. And no boy could be so strong. She had expected to see an invalid. Now it was manifest that the grip of those hands would be inescapable, and imagination suggested that those arms and shoulders could support the whole house. Miss Ironwood at her side struck her as a little old woman, shrivelled and pale—a thing you could have blown away.

The sofa was placed on a kind of dais divided from the rest of the room by a step. She had an impression of massed hangings of blue—later, she saw that it was only a screen—behind the man, so that the effect was that of a throne room. She would have called it silly if, instead of seeing it, she had been told of it by another. Through the window she saw no trees nor hills nor shapes of other houses: only the level floor of mist, as if this man and she were perched in a blue tower overlooking the world.

Pain came and went in his face: sudden jabs of sickening and burning pain. But as lightning goes through the darkness and the darkness closes up again and shows no trace, so the tranquillity of this countenance swallowed up each shock of torture. How could she have thought him young? Or old either? It came over her, with a sensation of quick fear, that this face was of no age at all. She had (or so she had believed) disliked bearded faces except for old men with white hair. But that was because she had long since forgotten the imagined Arthur of her childhood—and the imagined Solomon too. Solomon—for the first time in many years the bright solar blend of king and lover and magician which hangs about that name stole back upon her mind. For the first time in all those years she tasted the word *King* itself with all linked associations of battle, marriage, priest-hood, mercy, and power. At that moment, as her eyes first rested on his face, Jane forgot who she was, and where, and her faint grudge against Grace Ironwood, and her more ob-scure grudge against Mark, and her childhood and her fa-ther's house. It was, of course, only for a flash. Next moment she was once more the ordinary social Jane, flushed and confused to find that she had been staring rudely (at least she hoped that rudeness would be the main impression produced) at a total stranger. But her world was unmade; she knew that. Anything might happen now.

Arthurian England

DURING LUNCH Dr. Dimble talked about the Arthurian leg-end. "It's really wonderful," he said, "how the whole thing hangs together, even in a late version like Malory's. You've noticed how there are two sets of characters? There's Gui-nevere and Launcelot and all those people in the centre: all very courtly and nothing particularly British about them. But then in the background—on the other side of Arthur, so to speak—there are all those *dark* people like Morgan and Morgawse, who are very British indeed and usually more or less hostile though they are his own relatives. Mixed up with magic. You remember that wonderful phrase, how Queen Morgan 'set all the country on fire with ladies that were enchantresses.' Merlin too, of course, is British, though not hostile. Doesn't it look very like a picture of Britain as it must have been on the eve of the invasion?"

"How do you mean, Dr. Dimble?" said Jane.

"Well, wouldn't there have been one section of society

that was almost purely Roman? People wearing togas and talking a Celticised Latin—something that would sound to us rather like Spanish: and fully Christian. But further up country, in the out-of-the way places, cut off by the forests, there would have been little courts ruled by real old British under-kings, talking something like Welsh, and practising a certain amount of the Druidical religion."

"And what would Arthur himself have been?" said Jane. It was silly that her heart should have missed a beat at the words "rather like Spanish."

"That's just the point," said Dr. Dimble. "One can imagine a man of the old British line, but also a Christian and a fully-trained general with Roman technique, trying to pull this whole society together and almost succeeding. There'd be jealousy from his own British family, and the Romanised section—the Launcelots and Lionels—would look down on the Britons. That'd be why Kay is always represented as a boor: he is part of the native strain. And always that under-tow, that tug back to Druidism."

"And where would Merlin be?"

"Yes. . . . He's the really interesting figure. Did the whole thing fail because he died so soon? Has it ever struck you what an odd creation Merlin is? He's not evil; yet he's a magician. He is obviously a druid; yet he knows all about the Grail. He's 'the devil's son'; but then Layamon goes out of his way to tell you that the kind of being who fathered Merlin needn't have been bad after all. You remember, 'There dwell in the sky many kinds of wights. Some of them are good, and some work evil'."

"It *is* rather puzzling. I hadn't thought of it before."

"I often wonder," said Dr. Dimble, "whether Merlin doesn't represent the last trace of something the later tradition has quite forgotten about—something that became impossible when the only people in touch with the supernatural were either white or black, either priests or sorcerers."

"What a horrid idea," said Mrs. Dimble, who had noticed that Jane seemed to be preoccupied. "Anyway, Merlin happened a long time ago if he happened at all and he's safely dead and buried under Bragdon Wood as every one of us knows."

"Buried but *not* dead, according to the story," corrected Dr. Dimble.

"Ugh!" said Jane involuntarily, but Dr. Dimble was musing aloud.

"I wonder what they *will find* if they start digging up that place for the foundations of their N.I.C.E.," he said.

"First mud and then water," said Mrs. Dimble. "That's why they can't really build it there."

"So you'd think," said her husband. "And if so, why should they want to come here at all? A little cockney like Jules is not likely to be influenced by any poetic fancy about Merlin's mantle having fallen on him!"

"Merlin's mantle indeed!" said Mrs. Dimble.

"Yes," said the Doctor, "it's a rum idea. I daresay some of his set would like to recover the mantle well enough. Whether they'll be big enough to fill it is another matter! I don't think they'd like it if the old man himself came back to life along with it."

The Backward Village

THEY WALKED ABOUT that village for two hours and saw with their own eyes all the abuses and anachronisms they came to destroy. They saw the recalcitrant and backward labourer and heard his views on the weather. They met the wastefully supported pauper in the person of an old man shuffling across the courtyard of the almshouses to fill a kettle, and the elderly *rentier* (to make matters worse, she had a fat old dog with her) in earnest conversation with the postman. It made Mark feel as he were on a holiday, for it was only on holidays that he had ever wandered about an English village. For that reason he felt pleasure in it. It did not quite escape him that the face of the backward labourer was rather more interesting than Cosser's and his voice a great deal more pleasing to the ear. The resemblance between the elderly *rentier* and Aunt Gilly (When had he last thought of *her?* Good Lord, that took one back.) did make him understand how it was possible to like that kind of person. All this did not in the least influence his sociological convictions. Even if he had been free from Belbury and wholly unambitious, it could not have done so, for his education had had the curious effect of making things that he read and wrote more real to him than things he saw. Statistics about agricultural labourers were the substance; any real ditcher, ploughman, or farmer's boy, was the shadow. Though he had never noticed it himself, he had a great reluctance, in his work, ever to use such words as "man" or "woman." He preferred to write about "vocational groups," "elements," "classes" and "populations": for, in his own way, he believed as firmly as any mystic in the superior reality of the things that are not seen.

A Hross *Village*

EVER SINCE HE AWOKE on the space-ship Ransom had been thinking about the amazing adventure of going to another planet, and about his chances of returning from it. What he had not thought about was *being* on it. It was with a kind of stupefaction each morning that he found himself neither arriving in, nor escaping from, but simply living on, Malacandra; waking, sleeping, eating, swimming and even, as the days passed, talking. The wonder of it smote him most strongly when he found himself, about three weeks after his arrival, actually going for a walk. A few weeks later he had his favourite walks, and his favourite foods; he was beginning to develop habits. He knew a male from a female *hross* at sight, and even individual differences were becoming plain. Hyoi who had first found him—miles away to the north—was a very different person from the grey-muzzled, venerable Hnohra who was daily teaching him the language; and the young of the species were different again. They were delightful. You could forget all about the rationality of *hrossa* in dealing with them. Too young to trouble him with the baffling enigma of reason in an inhuman form, they solaced his loneliness, as if he had been allowed to bring a few dogs with him from the Earth. The cubs, on their part, felt the liveliest interest in the hairless goblin which had appeared among them. With them, and therefore indirectly with their dams, he was a brilliant success.

Of the community in general his earlier impressions were all gradually being corrected. His first diagnosis of their culture was what he called "old stone age." The few cutting instruments they possessed were made of stone. They seemed to have no pottery but a few clumsy vessels used for boiling, and boiling was the only cookery they attempted. Their common drink vessel, dish and ladle all in one, was the oyster-like shell in which he had first tasted *hross* hospitality; the fish which it contained was their only animal food. Vegetable fare they had in great plenty and variety, some of it delicious. Even the pinkish-white weed which covered the whole *handramit* was edible at a pinch, so that if he had starved before Hyoi found him he would have starved amidst abundance. No *hross*, however, ate the weed (*honodraskrud*) for choice, though it might be used *faute de mieux* on a journey. Their dwellings were beehive-shaped huts of stiff leaf and the villages—there were several in the neighbourhood—were always built beside rivers for warmth and well upstream towards the walls of the *handramit* where the water was hottest. They slept on the ground. They seemed to have no arts except a kind of poetry and music which was practised almost every evening by a team or troupe of four *hrossa*. One recited half chanting at great length while the other three, sometimes singly and sometimes antiphonally, interrupted him from time to time with song. Ransom could not find out whether these interruptions were simply lyrical interludes or dramatic dialogue arising out of the leader's narrative. He could make nothing of the music. The voices were not disagreeable and the scale seemed adapted to human ears, but the time-pattern was meaningless to his sense of rhythm. The occupations of the tribe or family were at first mysterious. People were always disappearing for a few days and reappearing again. There was a little fishing and much journeying in boats of which he never discovered the object. Then one day he saw a kind of caravan of *hrossa* setting out by land each with a load of vegetable food on its head. Apparently there was some kind of trade in Malacandra.

He discovered their agriculture in the first week. About a mile down the *handramit* one came to broad lands free of forest and clothed for many miles together in low pulpy vegetation in which yellow, orange and blue predominated. Later on, there were lettuce-like plants about the height of a terrestrial birch-tree. Where one of these overhung the warmth of water you could step into one of the lower leaves and lie deliciously as in a gently moving, fragrant hammock. Elsewhere it was not warm enough to sit still for long out of doors; the general temperature of the *handramit* was that of a fine winter's morning on Earth. These food-producing areas were worked communally by the surrounding villages, and division of labour had been carried to a higher point than he expected. Cutting, drying, storing, transport and something like manuring were all carried on, and he suspected that some at least of the water channels were artificial.

But the real revolution in his understanding of the *hrossa* began when he had learned enough of their language to attempt some satisfaction of their curiosity about himself. In answer to their questions he began by saying that he had come out of the sky. Hnohra immediately asked from which planet or earth (*handra*). Ransom, who had deliberately given a childish version of the truth in order to adapt it to the supposed ignorance of his audience, was a little annoyed to find Hnohra painfully explaining to him that he could not live in the sky because there was no air in it; he might have come through the sky but he must have come from a *handra*. He was quite unable to point Earth out to them in the night sky. They seemed surprised at his inability, and repeatedly pointed out to him a bright planet low on the western horizon—a little south of where the sun had gone down. He was surprised that they selected a planet instead of a mere star and stuck to their choice; could it be possible that they understood astronomy? Unfortunately he still knew too little of the language to explore their knowledge. He turned the conversation by asking them the name of the bright southern planet, and was told that it was Thulcandra—the silent world or planet.

"Why do you call it *Thulc?*" he asked. "Why silent?" No one knew.

"The *séroni* know," said Hnohra. "That is the sort of thing they know."

Hnakrapunt

"ONCE AN *eldil* has spoken," began Hyoi, when suddenly Whin gave a great cry (a "bark" Ransom would have called it three weeks ago) and pointed. There, not a furlong away, was the torpedo-like track of foam; and now, visible through a wall of foam, they caught the metallic glint of the monster's sides. Whin was paddling furiously. Hyoi threw and missed. As his first spear smote the water his second was already in the air. This time it must have touched the *hnakra*. He wheeled right out of the current. Ransom saw the great black pit of his mouth twice open and twice shut with its snap of shark-like teeth. He himself had thrown now—hurriedly, excitedly, with unpractised hand.

"Back," shouted Hyoi to Whin who was already backing water with every pound of his vast strength. Then all became confused. He heard Whin shout "Shore!" There came a shock that flung him forward almost into the *hnakra's* jaws and he found himself at the same moment up to his waist in water. It was at him the teeth were snapping. Then as he flung shaft after shaft into the great cavern of the gaping brute he saw Hyoi perched incredibly on its back—on its nose—bending forward and hurling from there. Almost at once the *hross* was dislodged and fell with a wide splash nearly ten yards away. But the *hnakra* was killed. It was wallowing on its side, bubbling out its black life. The water around him was dark and stank.

When he recollected himself they were all on shore, wet, steaming, trembling with exertion and embracing one another. It did not now seem strange to him to be clasped to a breast of wet fur. The breath of the *hrossa* which, though sweet, was not human breath, did not offend him. He was one with them. That difficulty which they, accustomed to more than one rational species, had perhaps never felt, was now overcome. They were all *hnau*. They had stood shoulder to shoulder in the face of an enemy, and the shapes of their heads no longer mattered. And he, even Ransom, had come through it and not been disgraced. He had grown up.

They were on a little promontory free of forest, on which they had run aground in the confusion of the fight. The wreckage of the boat and the corpse of the monster lay confused together in the water beside them. No sound from the rest of the hunting party was audible; they had been almost a mile ahead when they met the *hnakra*. All three sat down to recover their breath.

"So," said Hyoi, "we are *hnakrapunti*. This is what I have wanted all my life."

Civilization and Savagery

THE LAST OF THE WINE

You think if we sigh, drinking the last decanter,
We're sensual topers, and thence you are ready to prose
And read your lecture. Need you? Why should you banter
Or badger us? Better imagine it thus; suppose

A man to have come from Atlantis eastward sailing—
Lemuria has fallen in the fury of a tidal wave,
The cities are drowned, the pitiless all-prevailing
Inhuman sea is Numinor's salt grave.

To Europe he comes from Lemuria, saved from the wreck
Of the gilded, loftily builded, countless fleet
With the violet sails. A phial hangs from his neck,
Holding the last of a golden cordial, subtle and sweet.

Unnamed is Europe, untamed; wet desolation
Of unwelcoming woods, the elk, the mammoth and the
    bear,
The fen and the forest. Men of a barbarous nation
On the sand in a circle standing await him there.

Horribly ridged are their foreheads. Weapons of bone,
Unhandy and blunt, they brandish in their clumsy grips.
Their females set up a screaming, their bagpipes drone;
They gaze and mumble. He raises the flask to his lips.

It brings to his mind the strings, the flutes, the tabors,
How he drank with poets at the banquet, robed and
    crowned,

He recalls the pillared halls carved with the labours
Of curious masters, (Lemuria's cities lie drowned),

The festal nights; the jest that flashed for a second
Light as a bubble, bright with a thousand years
Of nurture; the honour and virtue, the grace unreckoned
That sat like a robe on the Atlantean peers.

It has made him remember ladies, proud glances,
Fearless and peerless beauty, flower-like hair,
Ruses and mockery, the music of grave dances
(Where musicians played, huge fishes goggle and stare).

He sighs, like us; then rises and turns to meet
Those naked men. Will they make him their spoil and prey
Or salute him as god and brutally fawn at his feet?
And which would be worse? He pitches the phial away.

Deeper into the Unconscious

I FOLLOWED HIM down the stair (the whole palace was empty) and we went into the Pillar Room. He looked all round him, and I became very afraid because I felt sure he was looking for that mirror of his. But I had given it to Redival when she became Queen of Phars; and what would he do to me when he learned that I had stolen his favourite treasure? But he went to one corner of the room and found there (which were strange things to find in such a place) two pickaxes and a crowbar. "To your work, goblin," he said, and made me take one of the picks. He began to break up the paved floor in the center of the room, and I helped him. It was very hard labour because of the pain in my back. When we had lifted four or five of the big stone flags we found a dark hole, like a wide well, beneath them.

"Throw yourself down," said the King, seizing me by the hand. And however I struggled, I could not free myself, and we both jumped together. When we had fallen a long way we alighted on our feet, nothing hurt by our fall. It was warmer down here and the air was hard to breathe, but it was not so dark that I could not see the place we were in. It was another Pillar Room, exactly like the one we had left, except that it was smaller and all made (floor, walls, and pillars) of raw earth. And here also my father looked about him, and once again I was afraid he would ask what I had done with his mirror. But instead, he went into a corner of the earthen room and there found two spades and put one into my hand and said, "Now, work. Do you mean to slug abed all your life?" So then we had to dig a hole in the center of the room. And this time the labour was worse than before, for what we dug was all tough, clinging clay, so that you had rather to cut it out in squares with the spade than to dig it. And the place was stifling. But at last we had done so much that another black hole opened beneath us. This time I knew what he meant to do to me, so I tried to keep my hand from his. But he caught it and said,

"Do you begin to set your wits against mine? Throw yourself down."

"Oh no, no, no; no further down; mercy!" said I.

"There's no Fox to help you here," said my father. "We're far below any dens that foxes can dig. There's hundreds of tons of earth between you and the deepest of them." Then we leaped down into the hole, and fell further than before, but again alighted unhurt. It was far darker here, yet I could see that we were in yet another Pillar Room; but this was of living rock, and water trickled down the walls of it. Though it was so like the two shallower rooms, this was far the smallest. And as I looked I could see that it was getting smaller still. The roof was closing in on us. I tried to cry out to him, "If you're not quick, we shall be buried," but I was smothering and no voice came from me. Then I thought, "He doesn't care. It's nothing for him to be buried, for he's dead already."

A Different Kind of Time

LUCY RAN OUT of the empty room into the passage and found the other three.

"It's all right," she repeated, "I've come back."

"What on earth are you talking about, Lucy?" asked Susan.

"Why?" said Lucy in amazement, "haven't you all been wondering where I was?"

"So you've been hiding, have you?" said Peter. "Poor old Lu, hiding and nobody noticed! You'll have to hide longer than that if you want people to start looking for you."

"But I've been away for hours and hours," said Lucy.

The others all stared at one another.

"Batty!" said Edmund tapping his head. "Quite batty."

"What do you mean, Lu?" asked Peter.

"What I said," answered Lucy. "It was just after breakfast when I went into the wardrobe, and I've been away for hours and hours, and had tea, and all sorts of things have happened."

"Don't be silly, Lucy," said Susan. "We've only just come out of that room a moment ago, and you were there then."

"She's not being silly at all," said Peter, "she's just making up a story for fun, aren't you, Lu? And why shouldn't she?"

"No, Peter, I'm not," she said. "It's—it's a magic wardrobe. There's a wood inside it, and it's snowing, and there's a Faun and a witch and it's called Narnia; come and see."

The others did not know what to think, but Lucy was so excited that they all went back with her into the room. She rushed ahead of them, flung open the door of the wardrobe and cried, "Now! go in and see for yourselves."

"Why, you goose," said Susan, putting her head inside and pulling the fur coats apart, "it's just an ordinary wardrobe, look! there's the back of it."

Then everyone looked in and pulled the coats apart; and they all saw—Lucy herself saw—a perfectly ordinary wardrobe. There was no wood and no snow, only the back of the wardrobe, with hooks on it. Peter went in and rapped his knuckles on it to make sure that it was solid.

"A jolly good hoax, Lu," he said as he came out again, "you have really taken us in, I must admit. We half believed you."

"But it wasn't a hoax at all," said Lucy, "really and truly. It was all different a moment ago. Honestly it was. I promise."

"Come, Lu," said Peter, "that's going a bit far. You've had your joke. Hadn't you better drop it now?"

Lucy grew very red in the face and tried to say something, though she hardly knew what she was trying to say, and burst into tears.

For the next few days she was very miserable. She could have made it up with the others quite easily at any moment if she could have brought herself to say that the whole thing was only a story made up for fun. But Lucy was a very truthful girl and she knew that she was really in the right; and she could not bring herself to say this. The others who thought she was telling a lie, and a silly lie too, made her very unhappy. The two elder ones did this without meaning to do it, but Edmund could be spiteful, and on this occasion he was spiteful. He sneered and jeered at Lucy and kept on asking her if she'd found any other new countries in other cupboards all over the house. What made it worse was that these days ought to have been delightful. The weather was fine and they were out of doors from morning to night, bathing, fishing, climbing trees, birds' nesting, and lying in the heather. But Lucy could not properly enjoy any of it. And so things went on until the next wet day.

An End to Dualism

"THAT IS the fundamental paradox. The thing we are reaching forward to is what you would call God. The reaching forward, the dynamism, is what people like you always call the Devil. The people like me, who do the reaching forward, are always martyrs. You revile us, and by us come to your goal."

"Does that mean in plainer language that the things the Force wants you to do are what ordinary people call diabolical?"

"My dear Ransom, I wish you would not keep relapsing on to the popular level. The two things are only moments in the single, unique reality. The world leaps forward through great men and greatness always transcends mere moralism. When the leap has been made our 'diabolism' as you would call it becomes the morality of the next stage; but while we are making it, we are called criminals, heretics, blasphemers. . . ."

"How far does it go? Would you still obey the Life-Force if you found it prompting you to murder me?"

"Yes."

"Or to sell England to the Germans?"

"Yes."

"Or to print lies as serious research in a scientific periodical?"

"Yes."

"God help you!" said Ransom.

"You are still wedded to your conventionalities," said Weston. "Still dealing in abstractions. Can you not even conceive a total commitment—a commitment to something which utterly overrides all our petty ethical pigeon-holes?"

Ransom grasped at the straw. "Wait, Weston," he said abruptly. "That may be a point of contact. You say it's a total commitment. That is, you're giving up yourself. You're not out for your own advantage. No, wait half a second. This *is* the point of contact between your morality and mine. We both acknowledge——"

"Idiot," said Weston. His voice was almost a howl and he had risen to his feet. "Idiot," he repeated. "Can you understand nothing? Will you always try to press everything back into the miserable framework of your old jargon about self and self-sacrifice? That is the old accursed dualism in another form. There is no possible distinction in concrete thought between me and the universe. In so far as I am the conductor of the central forward pressure of the universe, I am it. Do you see, you timid, scruple-mongering fool? I *am* the Universe. I, Weston, am your God and your Devil. I call that Force into me completely. . . ."

Then horrible things began happening. A spasm like that preceding a deadly vomit twisted Weston's face out of recognition. As it passed, for one second something like the old Weston reappeared—the old Weston, staring with eyes of horror and howling, "Ransom, Ransom! For Christ's sake don't let them——" and instantly his whole body spun round as if he had been hit by a revolver-bullet and he fell to the earth, and was there rolling at Ransom's feet, slavering and chattering and tearing up the moss by handfuls. Gradually the convulsions decreased. He lay still, breathing heavily, his eyes open but without expression. Ransom was kneeling beside him now. It was obvious that the body was alive, and Ransom wondered whether this were a stroke or an epileptic fit, for he had never seen either. He rummaged among the packages and found a bottle of brandy which he uncorked and applied to the patient's mouth. To his consternation the teeth opened, closed on the neck of the bottle and bit it through. No glass was spat out. "O God, I've killed him," said Ransom. But beyond a spurt of blood at the lips there was no change in his appearance. The face suggested that either he was in no pain or in pain beyond all human comprehension. Ransom rose at last, but before doing so he plucked the revolver from Weston's belt, then, walking down to the beach, he threw it as far as he could into the sea.

Faith Healing

IT WAS PSYCHE who nursed the Fox, however often forbidden. She would fight, yes, and bite, any who stood between her and his door; for she, too, had our father's hot blood, though her angers were all the sort that come from love. The Fox won through his illness, thinner and greyer than before. Now mark the subtlety of the god who is against us. The story of his recovery and Psyche's nursing got abroad; Batta alone was conduit-pipe enough, and there were a score of other talkers. It became a story of how the beautiful princess could cure the fever by her touch; soon, that her touch was the only thing that could cure it. Within two days half the city was at the palace gate—such scarecrows, risen from their beds, old dotards as eager to save their lives as if their lives in any event were worth a year's purchase, babies, sick men half-dead and carried on beds. I stood looking at them from behind barred windows, all the pity and dread of it, the smell of sweat and fever and garlic and foul clothes.

"The Princess Istra," they cried. "Send out the Princess with her healing hands. We die! Healing, healing, healing!"

"And bread," came other voices. "The royal granaries! We are starving."

This was at first, while they stood a little way off from the gate. But they got nearer. Soon they were hammering at it. Someone was saying, "Bring fire." But, behind them, the weaker voices wailed on, "Heal us, heal us. The Princess with the healing hands!"

"She'll have to go out," said my father. "We can't hold them." (Two-thirds of our guards were down with the fever.)

"Can she heal them?" said I to the Fox. "Did she heal you?"

"It is possible," said the Fox. "It might be in accordance with nature that some hands can heal. Who knows?"

"Let me go out," said Psyche. "They are our people."

"Our rump!" said my father. "They shall smart for this day's work if ever I get the whip hand of them again. But quick. Dress the girl. She has beauty enough, that's one thing. And spirit."

They put a queen's dress on her and a chaplet on her head and opened the door. You know how it is when you shed few tears or none, but there is a weight and pressure of weeping through your whole head. It is like that with me even now when I remember her going out, slim and straight as a sceptre, out of the darkness and cool of the hall into the hot, pestilential glare of that day. The people drew back, thrusting one another, the moment the doors opened. I think they expected a rush of spearmen. But a minute later the wailing and shouting died utterly away. Every man (and many a woman too) in that crowd was kneeling. Her beauty, which most of them had never seen, worked on them as a terror might work. Then a low murmur, almost a sob, began; swelled, broke into the gasping cry, "A goddess, a goddess." One woman's voice rang out clear. "It is Ungit herself in mortal shape."

Psyche went on, walking slowly and gravely, like a child

going to say a lesson, right in among all the foulness. She touched and she touched. They fell at her feet and kissed her feet and the edge of her robe and her shadow and the ground where she had trodden. And still she touched and touched. There seemed to be no end of it; the crowd increased instead of diminishing. For hours she touched. The air was stifling even for us who stood in the shadow of the porch. The whole earth and air ached for the thunderstorm which (we knew now) would not come. I saw her growing paler and paler. Her walk had become a stagger.

"King," said I, "it will kill her."

"Then more's the pity," said the King. "They'll kill us all if she stops."

It was over in the end, somewhere about sunset. We carried her to her bed, and next day the fever was on her. But she won through it. In her wanderings she talked most of her gold and amber castle on the ridge of the Grey Mountain. At her worst, there was no look of death upon her face. It was as if he dared not come near her. And when her strength came back she was more beautiful than before. The childishness had gone. There was a new and severer radiance. "Ah, no wonder," sang the Fox, "if the Trojans and the Achaeans suffer long woes for such a woman. Terribly does she resemble an undying spirit."

Earth's Evil Emissary

RANSOM SAW that a small black object had detached itself from the space-ship and was beginning to move uncertainly away from it. It puzzled him for a moment. Then it dawned on him that Weston—if it was Weston—probably knew the watery surface he had to expect on Venus and had brought some kind of collapsible boat. But could it be that he had not reckoned with tides or storms and did not foresee that it might be impossible for him ever to recover the spaceship? It was not like Weston to cut off his own retreat. And Ransom certainly did not wish Weston's retreat to be cut off. A Weston who could not, even if he chose, return to Earth, was an insoluble problem. Anyway, what could he, Ransom, possibly do without support from the eldila? He began to smart under a sense of injustice. What was the good of sending him—a mere scholar—to cope with a situation of this sort? Any ordinary pugilist, or, better still, any man who could make good use of a tommy-gun, would have been more to the purpose. If only they could find this King whom the Green Woman kept on talking about. . . .

But while these thoughts were passing through his mind he became aware of a dim murmuring or growling sound which had gradually been encroaching on the silence for some time. "Look," said the Lady suddenly, and pointed to the mass of islands. Their surface was no longer level. At the same moment he realised that the noise was that of waves: small waves as yet, but definitely beginning to foam on the rocky headlands of the Fixed Island. "The sea is rising," said the Lady. "We must go down and leave this land at once. Soon the waves will be too great—and I must not be here by night."

"Not that way," shouted Ransom. "Not where you will meet the man from my world."

"Why?" said the Lady. "I am Lady and Mother of this world. If the King is not here, who else should greet a stranger?"

"I will meet him."

"It is not your world, Piebald," she replied.

"You do not understand," said Ransom. "This man—he is a friend of that eldil of whom I told you—one of those who cling to the wrong good."

"Then I must explain it to him," said the Lady. "Let us go and make him older," and with that she slung herself down the rocky edge of the plateau and began descending the mountain slope. Ransom took longer to manage the rocks; but once his feet were again on the turf he began running as fast as he could. The Lady cried out in surprise as he flashed past her, but he took no notice. He could now see clearly which bay the little boat was making for and his attention was fully occupied in directing his course and making sure of his feet. There was only one man in the boat. Down and down the long slope he raced. Now he was in a fold: now in a winding valley which momentarily cut off the sight of the sea. Now at last he was in the cove itself. He glanced back and saw to his dismay that the Lady had also been running and was only a few yards behind. He glanced forward again. There were waves, though not yet very large ones, breaking on the pebbly beach. A man in shirt and shorts and a pith helmet was ankle-deep in the water, wading ashore and pulling after him a little canvas punt. It was certainly Weston, though his face had something about it which seemed subtly unfamiliar. It seemed to Ransom of vital importance to prevent a meeting between Weston and the Lady. He had seen Weston murder an inhabitant of Malacandra. He turned back, stretching out both arms to bar her way and shouting "Go back!" She was too near. For a second she was almost in his arms. Then she stood back from him, panting from the race, surprised, her mouth opened to speak. But at that moment he heard Weston's voice, from behind him, saying in English, "May I ask you, Dr. Ransom, what is the meaning of this?"

The Voice of the Tempter

"I AM WONDERING," said the woman's voice, "whether all the people of your world have the habit of talking about the same thing more than once. I have said already that we are forbidden to dwell on the Fixed Land. Why do you not either talk of something else or stop talking?"

"Because this forbidding is such a strange one," said the Man's voice. "And so unlike the ways of Maleldil in my world. And He has not forbidden you to think about dwelling on the Fixed Land."

"That would be a strange thing—to think about what will never happen."

"Nay, in our world we do it all the time. We put words together to mean things that have never happened and places that never were: beautiful words, well put together. And then tell them to one another. We call it stories or poetry. In that old world you spoke of, Malacandra, they did the same. It is for mirth and wonder and wisdom."

"What is the wisdom in it?"

"Because the world is made up not only of what is but of what might be. Maleldil knows both and wants us to know both."

"This is more that I ever thought of. The other—the Piebald one—has already told me things which made me feel like a tree whose branches were growing wider and wider apart. But this goes beyond all. Stepping out of what is into what might be and talking and making things out there . . . alongside the world. I will ask the King what he thinks of it."

"You see, that is what we always come back to. If only you had not been parted from the King."

"Oh, I see. That also is one of the things that might be. The world might be so made that the King and I were never parted."

"The world would not have to be different—only the way you live. In a world where people live on the Fixed Lands they do not become suddenly separated."

"But you remember we are not to live on the Fixed Land."

"No, but He has never forbidden you to think about it.

Might not that be one of the reasons why you are forbidden to do it—so that you may have a Might Be to think about, to make Story about as we call it?"

"I will think more of this. I will get the King to make me older about it."

"How greatly I desire to meet this King of yours! But in the matter of Stories he may be no older than you himself."

"That saying of yours is like a tree with no fruit. The King is always older than I, and about all things."

"But Piebald and I have already made you older about certain matters which the King never mentioned to you. That is the new good which you never expected. You thought you would always learn all things from the king; but now Maleldil has sent you other men whom it had never entered your mind to think of and they have told you things the King himself could not know."

"I begin to see now why the King and I were parted at this time. This is a strange and great good He intended for me."

"And if you refused to learn things from me and kept on saying you would wait and ask the King, would that not be like turning away from the fruit you had found to the fruit you had expected?"

"These are deep questions, Stranger. Maleldil is not putting much into my mind about them."

"Do you not see why?"

"No."

"Since Piebald and I have come to your world we have put many things into your mind which Maleldil has not. Do you not see that He is letting go of your hand a little?"

"How could He? He is wherever we go."

"Yes, but in another way. He is making you older—making you to learn things not straight from Him but by your own meetings with other people and your own questions and thoughts."

"He is certainly doing that."

"Yes. He is making you a full woman, for up till now you were only half made—like the beasts who do nothing of themselves. This time, when you meet the King again, it is you who will have things to tell him. It is you who will be older than he and who will make him older."

"Maleldil would not make a thing like that happen. It would be like a fruit with no taste."

"But it would have a taste for *him*. Do you not think the King must sometimes be tired of being the older? Would he not love you more if you were wiser than he?"

"Is this what you call a Poetry or do you mean that it really is?"

"I mean a thing that really is."

"But how could anyone love anything more? It is like saying a thing could be bigger than itself."

"I only meant you could become more like the women of my world."

"What are they like?"

"They are of a great spirit. They always reach out their hands for the new and unexpected good, and see that it is good long before the men understand it. Their minds run ahead of what Maleldil has told them. They do not need to wait for Him to tell them what is good, but know it for themselves as He does. They are, as it were, little Maleldils. And because of their wisdom, their beauty is as much greater than yours as the sweetness of these gourds surpasses the taste of water. And because of their beauty the love which the men have for them is as much greater than the King's love for you as the naked burning of Deep Heaven seen from my world is more wonderful than the golden roof of yours."

"I wish I could see them."

"I wish you could."

The Unman at Work

AT LAST HE GOT UP and resumed his walk. Next moment he
started and looked at the ground again. He quickened his
pace, and then once more stopped and looked. He stood
stock-still and covered his face. He called aloud upon
heaven to break the nightmare or to let him understand
what was happening. A trail of mutilated frogs lay along
the edge of the island. Picking his footsteps with care, he
followed it. He counted ten, fifteen, twenty: and the
twenty-first brought him to a place where the wood came
down to the water's edge. He went into the wood and came
out on the other side. There he stopped dead and stared.
Weston, still clothed but without his pith helmet, was
standing about thirty feet away: and as Ransom watched he
was tearing a frog—quietly and almost surgically inserting
his forefinger, with its long sharp nail, under the skin behind the creature's head and ripping it open. Ransom had
not noticed before that Weston had such remarkable nails.
Then he finished the operation, threw the bleeding ruin
away, and looked up. Their eyes met.

If Ransom said nothing, it was because he could not
speak. He saw a man who was certainly not ill, to judge
from his easy stance and the powerful use he had just been
making of his fingers. He saw a man who was certainly
Weston, to judge from his height and build and colouring
and features. In that sense he was quite recognisable. But
the terror was that he was also unrecognisable. He did not
look like a sick man: but he looked very like a dead one.
The face which he raised from torturing the frog had that
terrible power which the face of a corpse sometimes has of
simply rebuffing ever conceivable human attitude one can
adopt towards it. The expressionless mouth, the unwinking

stare of the eyes, something heavy and inorganic in the very folds of the cheek, said clearly: "I have features as you have, but there is nothing in common between you and me." It was this that kept Ransom speechless. What could you say—what appeal or threat could have any meaning— to *that*? And now, forcing its way up into consciousness, thrusting aside every mental habit and every longing not to believe, came the conviction that this, in fact, was not a man: that Weston's body was kept, walking and undecaying, in Perelandra by some wholly different kind of life, and that Weston himself was gone.

It looked at Ransom in silence and at last began to smile. We have all often spoken—Ransom himself had often spoken—of a devilish smile. Now he realised that he had never taken the words seriously. The smile was not bitter, nor raging, nor, in an ordinary sense, sinister; it was not even mocking. It seemed to summon Ransom, with horrible naïveté of welcome, into the world of its own pleasures, as if all men were at one in those pleasures, as if they were the most natural thing in the world and no dispute could ever have occurred about them. It was not furtive, nor ashamed, it had nothing of the conspirator in it. It did not defy goodness, it ignored it to the point of annihilation. Ransom perceived that he had never before seen anything but half-hearted and uneasy attempts at evil. This creature was whole-hearted. The extremity of its evil had passed beyond all struggle into some state which bore a horrible similarity to innocence. It was beyond vice as the Lady was beyond virtue.

The Devil

SATAN SPEAKS

I am Nature, the Mighty Mother,
I am the law: ye have none other.

I am the flower and the dewdrop fresh,
I am the lust in your itching flesh.

I am the battle's filth and strain,
I am the widow's empty pain.

I am the sea to smother your breath,
I am the bomb, the falling death.

I am the fact and the crushing reason
To thwart your fantasy's new-born treason.

I am the spider making her net,
I am the beast with jaws blood-wet.

I am a wolf that follows the sun
And I will catch him ere day be done.

The N.I.C.E.

THE MOST CONTROVERSIAL business before the College Meeting was the question of selling Bragdon Wood. The purchaser was the N.I.C.E., the National Institute of Coordinated Experiments. They wanted a site for the building which would worthily house this remarkable organisation. The N.I.C.E. was the first-fruits of that constructive fusion between the state and the laboratory on which so many thoughtful people base their hopes of a better world. It was to be free from almost all the tiresome restraints—"red tape" was the word its supporters used—which have hitherto hampered research in this country. It was also largely free from the restraints of economy, for, as it was argued, a nation which can spend so many millions a day on a war can surely afford a few millions a month on productive research in peacetime. The building proposed for it was one which would make a quite noticeable addition to the skyline of New York, the staff was to be enormous, and their salaries princely. Persistent pressure and endless diplomacy on the part of the Senate of Edgestow had lured the new Institute away from Oxford, from Cambridge, from London. It had thought of all these in turn as possible scenes for its labours. At times the Progressive Element in Edgestow had almost despaired. But success was now practically certain. If the N.I.C.E. could get the necessary land, it would come to Edgestow. And once it came, then, as everyone felt, things would at last begin to move. Curry had even expressed a doubt whether, eventually, Oxford and Cambridge could survive as major universities at all.

The N.I.C.E.

"I AGREE with James," said Curry, who had been waiting somewhat impatiently to speak. "The N.I.C.E. marks the beginning of a new era—the *really* scientific era. Up to now, everything has been haphazard. This is going to put science itself on a scientific basis. There are to be forty interlocking committees sitting every day and they've got a wonderful gadget—I was shown the model last time I was in town—by which the findings of each committee print themselves off in their own little compartment on the Analytical Notice-Board every half hour. Then, that report slides itself into the right position where it's connected up by little arrows with all the relevant parts of the other reports. A glance at the Board shows you the policy of the whole Institute actually taking shape under your own eyes. There'll be a staff of at least twenty experts at the top of the building working this Notice-Board in a room rather like the Tube control rooms. It's a marvellous gadget. The different kinds of business all come out in the Board in different coloured lights. It must have cost half a million. They call it a Pragmatometer."

"And there," said Busby, "you see again what the Institute is already doing for the country. Pragmatometry is going to be a big thing. Hundreds of people are going in for it. Why this Analytical Notice-Board will probably be out of date before the building is finished!"

"Yes, by Jove," said Feverstone, "and N.O. himself told me this morning that the sanitation of the Institute was going to be something quite out of the ordinary."

"So it is," said Busby sturdily. "I don't see why one should think that unimportant."

"And what do you think about it, Studdock?" said Feverstone.

"I think," said Mark, "that James touched on the most important point when he said that it would have its own legal staff and its own police. I don't give a fig for Pragmatometers and sanitation *de luxe*. The real thing is that this time we're going to get science applied to social problems and backed by the whole force of the state, just as war has been backed by the whole force of the state in the past. One hopes, of course, that it'll find out more than the old free-lance science did; but what's certain is that it can *do* more."

Cleaning the Planet Up

AT DINNER he sat next to Filostrato. There were no other members of the inner circle within earshot. The Italian was in good spirits and talkative. He had just given orders for the cutting down of some fine beech trees in the grounds.

"Why have you done that, Professor?" said a Mr. Winter who sat opposite. "I shouldn't have thought they did much harm at that distance from the house. I'm rather fond of trees myself."

"Oh, yes, yes," replied Filostrato. "The pretty trees, the garden trees. But not the savages. I put the rose in my garden, but not the brier. The forest tree is a weed. But I tell you I have seen the civilised tree in Persia. It was a French *attaché* who had it because he was in a place where trees do not grow. It was made of metal. A poor, crude thing. But how if it were perfected? Light, made of aluminium. So natural, it would even deceive."

"It would hardly be the same as a real tree," said Winter.

"But consider the advantages! You get tired of him in one place: two workmen carry him somewhere else: wherever you please. It never dies. No leaves to fall, no twigs, no birds building nests, no muck and mess."

"I suppose one or two, as curiosities, might be rather amusing."

"Why one or two? At present, I allow, we must have forests, for the atmosphere. Presently we find a chemical substitute. And then, why *any* natural trees? I foresee nothing but the *art* tree all over the earth. In fact, we *clean* the planet."

"Do you mean," put in a man called Gould, "that we are to have no vegetation at all?"

"Exactly. You shave your face: even, in the English fashion, you shave him every day. One day we shave the planet."

"I wonder what the birds will make of it?"

"I would not have any birds either. On the art tree I would have the art birds all singing when you press a switch inside the house. When you are tired of the singing you switch them off. Consider again the improvement. No feathers dropped about, no nests, no eggs, no dirt."

"It sounds," said Mark, "like abolishing pretty well all organic life."

"And why not? It is simple hygiene. Listen, my friends. If you pick up some rotten thing and find this organic life crawling over it, do you not say, 'Oh, the horrid thing. It is alive,' and then drop it?"

"Go on," said Winter.

"And you, especially you English, are you not hostile to any organic life except your own on your own body? Rather than permit it you have invented the daily bath."

"That's true."

"And what do you call dirty dirt? Is it not precisely the organic? Minerals are clean dirt. But the real filth is what comes from organisms—sweat, spittles, excretions. Is not your whole idea of purity one huge example? The impure and the organic are interchangeable conceptions."

"What are you driving at, Professor?" said Gould. "After all we are organisms ourselves."

"I grant it. That is the point. In us organic life has produced Mind. It has done its work. After that we want no more of it. We do not want the world any longer furred over with organic life, like what you call the blue mould—all sprouting and budding and breeding and decaying. We must get rid of it. By little and little, of course. Slowly we learn how. Learn to make our brains live with less and less body: learn to build our bodies directly with chemicals, no longer have to stuff them full of dead brutes and weeds. Learn how to reproduce ourselves without copulation."

"I don't think that would be much fun," said Winter.

"My friend, you have already separated the Fun, as you call it, from fertility. The Fun itself begins to pass away. Bah! I know that is not what you think. But look at your English women. Six out of ten are frigid, are they not? You see? Nature herself begins to throw away the anachronism. When she has thrown it away, then real civilisation becomes possible. You would understand if you were peasants. Who would try to work with stallions and bulls? No, no; we want geldings and oxen. There will never be peace and order and discipline so long as there is sex. When man has thrown it away, then he will become finally governable."

Babel

To DIFFERENT members of the audience the change came differently. To Frost it began at the moment when he heard Jules end a sentence with the words, "as gross an anachronism as to trust to Calvary for salvation in modern war." *Cavalry*, thought Frost almost aloud. Why couldn't the fool mind what he was saying? The blunder irritated him extremely. Perhaps—but hullo! what was this? Had his hearing gone wrong? For Jules seemed to be saying that the future density of mankind depended on the implosion of the horses of Nature. "He's drunk," thought Frost. Then, crystal clear in articulation, beyond all possibility of mistake, came, "The madrigore of verjuice must be talthibianised."

Wither was slower to notice what was happening. He had never expected the speech to have any meaning as a whole and for a long time the familiar catch-words rolled on in a manner which did not disturb the expectation of his ear. He thought, indeed, that Jules was sailing very near the wind, that a very small false step would deprive both the speaker and the audience of the power even to pretend that he was saying anything in particular. But as long as that border was not crossed, he rather admired the speech; it was in his own line. Then he thought, "Come! That's going too far. Even they must see that you can't talk about accepting the challenge of the past by throwing down the gauntlet of the future." He looked cautiously down the room. All was well. But it wouldn't be if Jules didn't sit down pretty soon. In that last sentence there were surely words he didn't know. What the deuce did he mean by *aholibate*? He looked down the room again. They were attending too much, always a bad sign. Then came the sentence, "The surrogates esemplanted in a continual of porous variations."

The Intervention of the Animals

ABOVE THE CHAOS of sounds which now awoke—there seemed to be a new animal in the room every minute—there came at last one sound in which those still capable of understanding could take comfort. *Thud—thud—thud;* the door was being battered from the outside. It was a huge folding door, a door by which a small locomotive could almost enter, for the room was made in imitation of Versailles. Already one or two of the panels were splintering. The noise maddened those who had made that door their goal. It seemed also to madden the animals. They did not stop to eat what they killed, or not more than to take one lick of the blood. There were dead and dying bodies everywhere by now, for the scrum was by this time killing as many as the beasts. And always from all sides went up the voices trying to shout to those beyond the door. "Quick. Quick. Hurry," but shouting only nonsense. Louder and louder grew the noise at the door. As if in imitation a great gorilla leaped on the table where Jules had sat and began drumming on its chest. Then, with a roar, it jumped down into the crowd.

At last the door gave. Both wings gave. The passage, framed in the doorway, was dark. Out of the darkness there came a grey snaky something. It swayed in the air; then began methodically to break off the splintered wood on each side and make the doorway clear. Then Mark saw distinctly how it swooped down, curled itself round a man— Steele, he thought, but everyone looked different now—and lifted him bodily high off the floor. After that, monstrous, improbable, the huge shape of the elephant thrust its way into the room: its eyes enigmatic, its ears standing stiffly out like the devil's wings on each side of its head. It stood for a second with Steele writhing in the curl of its trunk and then dashed him to the floor. It trampled him. After it raised head and trunk again and brayed horribly; then plunged straight forward into the room, trumpeting and trampling—continuously trampling like a girl treading grapes, heavily and soon wetly tramping in a pash of blood and bones, of flesh, wine, fruit, and sodden tablecloth. Something more than danger darted from the sight into Mark's brain. The pride and insolent glory of the beast, the carelessness of its killings, seemed to crush his spirit even as its flat feet were crushing women and men. Here surely came the King of the world . . . then everything went black and he knew no more.

Damnation

STILL NOT ASKING what he would do or why, Frost went to the garage. The whole place was silent and empty; the snow was thick on the ground by this. He came up with as many petrol tins as he could carry. He piled all the inflammables he could think of together in the Objective Room. Then he locked himself in by locking the outer door of the ante-room. Whatever it was that dictated his actions then compelled him to push the key into the speaking tube which communicated with the passage. When he had pushed it as far in as his fingers could reach, he took a pencil from his pocket and pushed with that. Presently he heard the clink of the key falling on the passage floor outside. That tiresome illusion, his consciousness, was screaming to protest; his body, even had he wished, had no power to attend to those screams. Like the clockwork figure he had chosen to be, his stiff body, now terribly cold, walked back into the Objective Room, poured out the petrol and threw a lighted match into the pile. Not till then did his controllers allow him to suspect that death itself might not after all cure the illusion of being a soul—nay, might prove the entry into a world where that illusion raged infinite and unchecked. Escape for the soul, if not for the body, was offered him. He became able to know (and simultaneously refused the knowledge) that he had been wrong from the beginning, that souls and personal responsibility existed. He half saw: he wholly hated. The physical torture of the burning was not fiercer than his hatred of that. With one supreme effort he flung himself back into his illusion. In that attitude eternity overtook him as sunrise in old tales overtakes trolls and turns them into unchangeable stone.

The Barrage of the Enemy

THE FARTHER I WENT the more impossible I found it to think about anything except these eldila. What, after all, did Ransom really know about them? By his own account the sorts which he had met did not usually visit our own planet—or had only begun to do so since his return from Mars. We had eldila of our own, he said, Tellurian eldils, but they were of a different kind and mostly hostile to man. That, in fact, was why our world was cut off from communication with the other planets. He described us as being in a state of siege, as being, in fact, an enemy-occupied territory, held down by eldils who were at war both with us and with the eldils of "Deep Heaven," or "space." Like the bacteria on the microscopic level, so these co-inhabiting pests on the macroscopic permeate our whole life invisibly and are the real explanation of that fatal bent which is the main lesson of history. If all this were true, then, of course, we should welcome the fact that eldila of a better kind had at last broken the frontier (it is, they say, at the Moon's orbit) and were beginning to visit us. Always assuming that Ransom's account was the correct one.

A nasty idea occurred to me. Why should not Ransom be a dupe? If something from outer space were trying to invade our planet, what better smoke-screen could it put up than this very story of Ransom's? Was there the slightest evidence, after all, for the existence of the supposed maleficent eldils on this earth? How if my friend were the unwitting bridge, the Trojan Horse, whereby some possible invader were effecting its landing on Tellus? And then once more, just as when I had discovered that I had no pack, the impulse to go no farther returned to me. "Go back, go back," it whispered to me, "send him a wire, tell him you were ill, say you'll come some other time—anything." The strength of the feeling astonished me. I stood still for a few moments telling myself not to be a fool, and when I finally resumed my walk I was wondering whether this might be the beginning of a nervous breakdown. No sooner had this idea occurred to me than it also became a new reason for not visiting Ransom. Obviously, I wasn't fit for any such jumpy "business" as his telegram almost certainly referred to. I wasn't even fit to spend an ordinary week-end away from home. My only sensible course was to turn back at once and get safe home, before I lost my memory or became hysterical, and to put myself in the hands of a doctor. It was sheer madness to go on.

I was now coming to the end of the heath and going down a small hill, with a copse on my left and some apparently deserted industrial buildings on my right. At the bottom the evening mist was partly thick. "They call it a Breakdown *at first*," I thought. Wasn't there some mental disease in which quite ordinary objects looked to the patient unbelievably ominous? . . . looked, in fact, just as that abandoned factory looks to me now? Great bulbous shapes of cement, strange brickwork bogeys, glowered at me over dry scrubby grass pock-marked with grey pools and intersected with the remains of a light railway. I was reminded of things which Ransom had seen in that other world: only there, they were people. Long spindle-like giants whom he called Sorns. What made it worse was that he regarded them as good people—very much nicer, in fact, than our own race. He was in league with them! How did I know he was even a dupe? He might be something worse . . . and again I came to a standstill.

The reader, not knowing Ransom, will not understand how contrary to all reason this idea was. The rational part of my mind, even at that moment, knew perfectly well that even if the whole universe were crazy and hostile, Ransom was sane and wholesome and honest. And this part of my mind in the end sent me forward—but with a reluctance and a difficulty I can hardly put into words. What enabled me to go on was the knowledge (deep down inside me) that I was getting nearer at every stride to the one friend: but I *felt* that I was getting nearer to the one enemy—the traitor, the sorcerer, the man in league with "them". . . . walking into the trap with my eyes open, like a fool. "They call it a breakdown at first," said my mind, "and send you to a nursing home; later on they move you to an asylum."

Temptation

THE QUEEN took from somewhere among her wrappings a very small bottle which looked as if it were made of copper. Then, holding out her arm, she let one drop fall from it on to the snow beside the sledge. Edmund saw the drop for a second in mid-air, shining like a diamond. But the moment it touched the snow there was a hissing sound and there stood a jewelled cup full of something that steamed. The Dwarf immediately took this and handed it to Edmund with a bow and a smile; not a very nice smile. Edmund felt much better as he began to sip the hot drink. It was something he had never tasted before, very sweet and foamy and creamy, and it warmed him right down to his toes.

"It is dull, Son of Adam, to drink without eating," said the Queen presently. "What would you like best to eat?"

"Turkish Delight, please, your Majesty," said Edmund.

The Queen let another drop fall from her bottle on to the snow, and instantly there appeared a round box, tied with green silk ribbon, which, when opened, turned out to contain several pounds of the best Turkish Delight. Each piece was sweet and light to the very centre and Edmund had never tasted anything more delicious. He was quite warm now, and very comfortable.

While he was eating the Queen kept asking him questions. At first Edmund tried to remember that it is rude to speak with one's mouth full, but soon he forgot about this and thought only of trying to shovel down as much Turkish Delight as he could, and the more he ate the more he wanted to eat, and he never asked himself why the Queen should be so inquisitive. She got him to tell her that he had one brother and two sisters, and that one of his sisters had already been in Narnia and had met a Faun there, and that no one except himself and his brother and his sisters knew anything about Narnia. She seemed especially interested in the fact that there were four of them, and kept on coming back to it. "You are sure there are just four of you?" she asked. "Two Sons of Adam and two Daughters of Eve, neither more nor less?" and Edmund, with his mouth full of Turkish Delight, kept on saying, "Yes, I told you that before," and forgetting to call her "Your Majesty" but she didn't seem to mind now.

At last the Turkish Delight was all finished and Edmund was looking very hard at the empty box and wishing that she would ask him whether he would like some more. Probably the Queen knew quite well what he was thinking; for she knew, though Edmund did not, that this was enchanted Turkish Delight and that anyone who had once tasted it would want more and more of it, and would even, if they were allowed, go on eating it till they killed themselves. But she did not offer him any more. Instead, she said to him,

"Son of Adam, I should so much like to see your brother and your two sisters. Will you bring them to me?"

"I'll try," said Edmund, still looking at the empty box.

"Because, if you did come again—bringing them with you of course—I'd be able to give you some more Turkish

Delight. I can't do it now, the magic will only work once. In my own house it would be another matter."

"Why can't we go to your house now?" said Edmund. When he had first got on to the sledge he had been afraid that she might drive away with him to some unknown place from which he would not be able to get back, but he had forgotten about that fear now.

"It is a lovely place, my house," said the Queen. "I am sure you would like it. There are whole rooms full of Turkish Delight, and what's more, I have no children of my own. I want a nice boy whom I could bring up as a Prince and who would be King of Narnia when I am gone. While he was Prince he would wear a gold crown and eat Turkish Delight all day long; and you are much the cleverest and handsomest young man I've ever met. I think I would like to make you the Prince—some day, when you bring the others to visit me."

"Why not now?" said Edmund. His face had become very red and his mouth and fingers were sticky. He did not look either clever or handsome whatever the Queen might say.

Treason

ALL THE CHILDREN had been attending so hard to what Mr. Beaver was telling them that they had noticed nothing else for a long time. Then during the moment of silence that followed his last remark, Lucy suddenly said:

"I say—where's Edmund?"

There was a dreadful pause, and then everyone began asking "Who saw him last? How long has he been missing? Is he outside?" And then all rushed to the door and looked out. The snow was falling thickly and steadily, the green ice of the pool had vanished under a thick white blanket, and from where the little house stood in the centre of the dam you could hardly see either bank. Out they went, plunging well over their ankles into the soft new snow, and went round the house in every direction. "Edmund! Edmund!" they called till they were hoarse. But the silently falling snow seemed to muffle their voices and there was not even an echo in answer.

"How perfectly dreadful!" said Susan as they at last came back in despair. "Oh, how I wish we'd never come."

"What on earth are we to do, Mr. Beaver?" said Peter.

"Do?" said Mr. Beaver who was already putting on his snow boots, "do? We must be off at once. We haven't a moment to spare!"

"We'd better divide into four search parties," said Peter, "and all go in different directions. Whoever finds him must come back here at once and—"

"Search parties, Son of Adam?" said Mr. Beaver; "what for?"

"Why, to look for Edmund of course!"

"There's no point in looking for him," said Mr. Beaver.

"What do you mean?" said Susan, "he can't be far away yet. And we've got to find him. What do you mean when you say there's no use looking for him?"

"The reason there's no use looking," said Mr. Beaver, "is that we know already where he's gone!" Everyone stared in amazement. "Don't you understand?" said Mr. Beaver. "He's gone to *her*, to the White Witch. He has betrayed us all."

"Oh surely—oh really!" said Susan, "he can't have done that."

"Can't he?" said Mr. Beaver looking very hard at the three children, and everything they wanted to say died on their lips for each felt suddenly quite certain inside that this was exactly what Edmund had done.

"But will he know the way?" said Peter.

"Has he been in this country before?" asked Mr. Beaver, "has he ever been here alone?"

"Yes," said Lucy almost in a whisper, "I'm afraid he has."

"And did he tell you what he'd done or who he'd met?"

"Well, no, he didn't," said Peter.

"Then mark my words," said Mr. Beaver, "he has already met the White Witch and joined her side, and been told where she lives. I didn't like to mention it before (he being your brother and all) but the moment I set eyes on that brother of yours I said to myself 'Treacherous.' He had the look of one who has been with the Witch and eaten her food. You can always tell them if you've lived long in Narnia, something about their eyes."

The Great Dance

AND NOW, by a transition which he did not notice, it seemed that what had begun as speech was turned into sight, or into something that can be remembered only as if it were seeing. He thought he saw the Great Dance. It seemed to be woven out of the intertwining undulation of many cords or bands of light, leaping over and under one another and mutually embraced in arabesques and flower-like subtleties. Each figure as he looked at it became the master-figure or focus of the whole spectacle, by means of which his eye disentangled all else and brought it into unity—only to be itself entangled when he looked to what he had taken for mere marginal decorations and found that there also the same hegemony was claimed, and the claim made good, yet the former pattern not thereby dispossessed but finding in its new subordination a significance greater than that which it had abdicated. He could see also (but the word "seeing" is now plainly inadequate) wherever the ribbons or serpents of light intersected, minute corpuscles of momentary brightness: and he knew somehow that these particles were the secular generalities of which history tells—peoples, institutions, climates of opinion, civilisations, arts, sciences, and the like—ephemeral coruscations that piped their short song and vanished. The ribbons or cords themselves, in which millions of corpuscles lived and died, were things of some different kind. At first he could not say what. But he knew in the end that most of them were individual entities. If so, the time in which the Great Dance proceeds is very unlike time as we know it. Some of the thinner and more delicate cords were beings that we call short-lived: flowers and insects, a fruit or a storm of rain, and once (he thought) a wave of the sea. Others were such things as we also think lasting: crystals, rivers, mountains, or even stars. Far above these in girth and luminosity and flashing with colours from beyond our spectrum were the lines of the personal beings, yet as different from one another in splendour as all of them from the previous class. But not all the cords were individuals: some were universal truths or universal qualities. It did not surprise him then to find that these and the persons were both cords and both stood together as against the mere atoms of generality which lived and died in the clashing of their streams: but afterwards, when he came back to earth, he wondered. And by now the thing must have passed together out of the region of sight as we understand it. For he says that the whole solid figure of these enamoured and inter-inanimated circlings was suddenly revealed as the mere superficies of a far vaster pattern in four dimensions, and that figure as the boundary of yet others in other worlds: till suddenly as the movement grew yet swifter, the interweaving yet more ecstatic, the relevance of all to all yet more intense, as dimension was added to dimension and that part of him which could reason and remember was dropped farther and farther behind that part of him which saw, even then, at the very zenith of complexity, complexity was eaten up and faded, as a thin white cloud fades into the hard blue burning of the sky, and a simplicity beyond all comprehension, ancient and young as spring, illimitable, pellucid, drew him with cords of infinite desire into its own stillness. He went up into such a quietness, a privacy, and a freshness that at the very moment when he stood farthest from our ordinary mode of being he had the sense of stripping off encumbrances and awaking from trance, and coming to himself. With a gesture of relaxation he looked about him. . . .

Bibliography

BOOKS QUOTED IN THE TEXT

The Great Divorce
London: Geoffrey Bles, 1945
New York: Macmillan Publishing Co., Inc., 1946
New York: Macmillan Paperbacks, 1963
The Horse and His Boy. Book 5 in *The Chronicles of Narnia.*
Illustrated by Pauline Baynes
London: The Bodley Head, 1956
New York: Macmillan Publishing Co., Inc., 1954
New York: Collier Books, 1970
The Last Battle. Book 7 in *The Chronicles of Narnia.* Illustrated by
Pauline Baynes
London: The Bodley Head, 1956
New York: Macmillan Publishing Co., Inc., 1956
New York: Collier Books, 1970

The Lion, the Witch and the Wardrobe. Book 1 in *The Chronicles of Narnia*. Illustrated by Pauline Baynes
London: Geoffrey Bles, 1950
New York: Macmillan Publishing Co., Inc., 1950
New York: Collier Books, 1970
The Magician's Nephew, Book 6 in *The Chronicles of Narnia*. Illustrated by Pauline Baynes
London: The Bodley Head, 1955
New York: Macmillan Publishing Co., Inc., 1955
New York: Collier Books, 1970
Narrative Poems. Edited by Walter Hooper
London: Geoffrey Bles, 1969
New York: Harcourt Brace Jovanovich, 1972
Out of the Silent Planet. Book 1 of *The Space Trilogy*
London: John Lane, 1938
New York: Macmillan Publishing Co., Inc., 1943
New York: Macmillan Paperbacks, 1965
Perelandra. Book 2 of *The Space Trilogy*
London: John Lane, 1943
New York: Macmillan Publishing Co., Inc., 1944
New York: Macmillan Paperbacks, 1965
The Pilgrim's Regress: An Allegorical Apology for Christianity, Reason, and Romanticism
London: J. M. Dent, 1933
New York: Sheed and Ward, 1935
With the author's important new Preface on Romanticism, footnotes, and running headlines
London: Geoffrey Bles, 1943
New York: Sheed and Ward, 1944
Grand Rapids: W. B. Eerdmans Publishing Co., 1958
Poems. Edited by Walter Hooper
London: Geoffrey Bles, 1964
New York: Harcourt Brace Jovanovich, 1965
Prince Caspian. Book 2 in *The Chronicles of Narnia*. Illustrated by Pauline Baynes
London: Geoffrey Bles, 1951
New York: Macmillan Publishing Co., Inc., 1951
New York: Collier Books, 1970
The Screwtape Letters, with Screwtape Proposes a Toast. With a new and additional Preface
New York: Macmillan Publishing Co., Inc., 1964
New York: Macmillan Paperbacks, 1962

The Silver Chair. Book 4 in *The Chronicles of Narnia.* Illustrated by
   Pauline Baynes
   London: Geoffrey Bles, 1953
   New York: Macmillan Publishing Co., Inc., 1953
   New York: Collier Books, 1970
Spirits in Bondage: A Cycle of Lyrics (under pseudonym of Clive
   Hamilton)
   London: William Heinemann, 1919
   Ann Arbor: University Microfilms International, 1976
That Hideous Strength. Book 3 of *The Space Trilogy*
   London: John Lane, 1945
   New York: Macmillan Publishing Co., Inc., 1946
   New York: Macmillan Paperbacks, 1965
Till We Have Faces: A Myth Retold
   London: Geoffrey Bles, 1956
   New York: Harcourt Brace Jovanovich, 1957
   Grand Rapids: WBE Paperback, 1966
The Voyage of the Dawn Treader. Book 3 in *The Chronicles of Narnia.*
   Illustrated by Pauline Baynes
   London: Geoffrey Bles, 1952
   New York: Macmillan Publishing Co., Inc., 1952
   New York: Collier Books, 1970

Sources

The page numbers below refer to the American paperback editions of C. S. Lewis's works when these are available. For the benefit of readers with other editions, chapter numbers are given in parentheses.

The Agony of Aslan

> *The Lion, the Witch and the Wardrobe*, 145–148 (Ch. 14)

The Ageless Pendragon

> *That Hideous Strength*, 142–143 (Ch. 7)

The Anti-Romantics

> *The Pilgrim's Regress*, 97–98 (Book 6, Ch. 2)

The Apostate Bishop

> *The Great Divorce*, 43–46 (Ch. 5)

Arthurian England

> *That Hideous Strength*, 31–32 (Ch. 1)

At the Border of Heaven

> *The Great Divorce*, 24–28 (Ch. 3)